SEEING ORGANIZATIONAL PATTERNS

SEEING ORGANIZATIONAL PATTERNS

A New Theory and Language of Organizational Design

By ROBERT W. KEIDEL

BeardBooks
Washington, D.C.

Copyright ©1995 by Robert W. Keidel
Originally Published 1995 by Berrett-Koehler Publishers, Inc.
Reprinted 2005 by Beard Books, Washington, D.C.

ISBN 1-58798-259-5

Printed in the United States of America

To Carole, Andy, and Carly

C O N T E N T S

"If the patterns out of which a thing is made are alive,
then we shall see them over and over again,
just because they make sense."

—CHRISTOPHER ALEXANDER,
THE TIMELESS WAY OF BUILDING

A few years ago, my daughter—then eight years old—was asked by a
friend what her daddy did for a living. I overheard Carly reply, "He
helps businesses and draws triangles for them." That pretty much sums
up my professional life since the late 1980s. Or, more precisely, I have
tried to help organizations by drawing triangles *with* them—and, especially, enabling them to draw their own triangles.

Why triangles? Because this shape counterposes three critical
organizational variables: autonomy, control, and cooperation. By
learning how to frame issues as a balance of these variables, one can
see underlying patterns that had not been visible—and thereby make
more intelligent analyses, choices, and commitments than would
otherwise be possible.

Today, managers everywhere are bombarded by data from all directions. John Seely Brown, director of Xerox's Palo Alto Research Center, offers the following hypothesis about overload: "It may be that we feel we're drowning in information because the information we're getting doesn't easily fit into our current mental models for understanding the world. The knowledge economy is fundamentally different from the industrial economy, and we haven't begun to come to terms with how different these two economies are."[1] This book confronts the difference head on. Its premise is that those who can imaginatively and systematically think through organizational problems will have a strategic advantage over those who cannot.

Much of the organizational literature of the past several decades has been cast in terms of two variables. The most popular concepts have revolved around a single dyad: soft/hard—also expressed as social/technical, Theory Y/Theory X, relationship/task, people/production, organic/mechanistic, high-touch/high-tech, loose/tight, and so on. But the unmitigated press of competition, complexity, and change puts a premium on more sophisticated conceptualization. The time seems ripe for thinking in threes.

To be sure, not all organizational issues involve three variables. But since so many issues appear to be just such a triadic play, I have deliberately erred in the direction of commission rather than omission. In so doing, I have been encouraged by the words of physicist Frank Oppenheimer, who suggests that "If one has a new way of thinking, why not apply it wherever one's thought leads to? It is certainly entertaining to let oneself do so, but it is also often very illuminating and capable of leading to new and deep insights."[2]

Seeing Organizational Patterns is a "theory essay" intended for a broad class of organizational design professionals—encompassing academics, consultants, and managers. Yet I have written this book in the spirit of Kurt Lewin's famous dictum that "There is nothing so practical as a good theory."

Too often, when faced with serious organizational challenge, managers either become entangled in detail or try to escape the conundrum by trivializing. *Seeing Organizational Patterns* represents a third way that is neither unduly complicated nor simplistic.

Ultimately, the ideas presented here can clarify organizing by enabling managers to comprehend multiple perspectives, interactions, and consequences—and thus anticipate and avoid unforeseen pitfalls. Additionally, "triangulation" can spawn more opportunities, options, and connections than had been previously dreamt of.

The more that I have "played" with triangular thinking, the more unity has emerged out of seemingly disparate organizational characterizations. And it is becoming clearer every day that precious lessons for organizational designers reside in mathematics *and* science *and* architecture *and* art. At a fundamental level, I believe that organizational design should be a highly visual, even aesthetic activity. *Seeing Organizational Patterns* is my expression of this conviction.

THE BOOK'S STRUCTURE

Seeing Organizational Patterns is divided into three parts. Part 1, "Understanding Organizational Design," sets the context and presents the thesis that organizational design can usefully be understood in terms of triangular patterns. Chapter 1 introduces the concept of triadic organizational design. Chapter 2 locates the limitations of current design approaches in the thinking that underlies them. Chapter 3 shows how several organizations have effectively triangulated autonomy, control, and cooperation as an essential part of planning, design, and/or dialogue.

Part 2, "Framing Organizational Issues," presents an idealized diagnostic framework, the Organizational Design Profile, that fleshes out three internally-consistent designs—autonomy-based, control-based, and cooperation-based—across nine dimensions. Chapter 4 discusses organizational *strategy* across three of these dimensions: constituencies, character, and capabilities. Chapter 5 defines organizational *structure* across three additional dimensions: the organization chart, layout, and interdependence. Chapter 6 describes organizational *systems* in terms of three final dimensions: rewards, meetings, and decisions. Although in no way intended as a tool kit, chapters 4, 5, and 6 provide conceptual insights that can readily be converted into practical methods for organizational analysis.

Part 3, "Designing for Tomorrow," places *organizing* in conceptual and metaphorical perspective. Chapter 7 defines the concept of an *organizational pattern language*, identifies parallels between triangular design and other disciplines, and provides general guidelines for applying triangular design. Chapter 8 depicts a new organizational model, the *autonomy/cooperation hybrid*, that unifies a host of organizational analogies; and outlines current business examples of blending these two design variables.

Appendix A offers practical guidelines for using the Organizational Design Profile as a diagnostic framework. Appendix B lists more than 200 triads (from organization-related literatures, both academic and trade) that parallel autonomy/control/cooperation. This catalog provides theoretical support for the argument of *Seeing Organizational Patterns*. It also helps to integrate various concepts and writings that historically have remained fragmented.

This book represents both an integral whole and a set of relatively free-standing parts. Readers interested in only the essentials of my framework may choose to skip part 2 and the appendixes. Alternatively, those with an eye toward organizational diagnosis may find part 2 and appendix A of particular value. Finally, readers concerned about the relation between triangular design and contemporary organizational metaphors should find part 3 and appendix B provocative.

Wyncote, Pennsylvania   Robert W. Keidel
January 1995

ACKNOWLEDGMENTS

This book has been six years in the making. When I first broached the idea to my then-literary agent, the late Peter Livingston, I received a simple rejoinder: "Thinking books don't sell." Despite Peter's reservations, Barrie Van Dyck, my current agent, has patiently responded to several iterations of what has become a statement about thinking *about organizational design*.

As much as anyone else, Vinnie Carroll of the Center for Applied Research is responsible for my composing *Seeing Organizational Patterns*. In 1989, Vinnie convinced me to trade in my personal computer for a Macintosh; since then, I have spent at least as much time rendering as I have writing. I am at the point now that if I can't draw it, I don't get it.

My liberal arts education at Williams College certainly contributed to this words-and-pictures perspective; John Chandler, in particular, provided critical support—and still does. At Wharton, Eric Trist became my mentor, colleague, and friend. A bridge-builder of unparalleled scope, his life defined what it means to be "variety-increasing." In his last years, Eric strongly encouraged me to publish the organizational ideas that have come together in this book.

I owe a significant debt to a small group of friends and colleagues who have never tired (or let on that they were tired) of my triangles and tribulations. John Eldred, Tom Gilmore, Greg Shea, and Michael Umen have consistently provided comments that were candid, considerate, and constructive. So has my brother-in-law, Tom Zitrides—an uncommon entrepreneur who is equally pragmatic and reflective.

I have also been fortunate to work with several clients who could see practical as well as theoretical value in my ideas. In particular, George Lutzow, Barbara Marinan, and Ian Scott have each taken a few core premises and articulated them in ways that I could never have imagined; they have created their own frames, icons, and languages. And Ben Thorp has been a stimulating reviewer/collaborator for several years.

Other clients who have provided helpful perspectives on my work include Ron Budzinski, Tom Carter, Louis de Merode, Alan Hoffmann, Henry Hofmann, Jim Kochanski, Bruce Kowalski, Keith Otto, Bob Picciotto, and Frank Vitetta.

Thanks to a number of individuals who either reviewed earlier drafts or thoughtfully critiqued ideas in this book—namely, Russ Ackoff, Vic Baxter, Lee Bolman, Joel DeLuca, Bill Evan, Barbara Feinberg, Marlena Fiol, Janet Greco, Don Hambrick, Jim Hartling, Steve Lorch, Sue McKibbin, Howard Perlmutter, Dave Pierson, Lance Rosemore, Michael Schrage, Bob Shaw, Art Shostak, Linda Smircich, Bill Smith, Gerry Susman, Lee Evan Tabas, Ram Tenkasi, John Turchi, Bill Whyte, Tom Wieckowski, and Joan Weiner. I also appreciate the willingness of Harold Burlingame, Hesh Kestin, Diana Thompson, and Charles Wang to verify, and expand, the details of cases that presage a new organizational form.

Steve Piersanti, founder and president of Berrett-Koehler, deserves far more than a paragraph. He took a flier on a set of concepts and constructs that many others saw little future in. He found patterns in my work that I had missed—and then uncannily came up with the right book title. Steve has also proven to be a skillful yet author-friendly editor. *Seeing Organizational Patterns* is worlds better because of his contributions.

I also want to thank Jim Bell and Randy Moore for effectively managing the conversion of raw manuscript into finished product.

Closer to home, thanks to my parents, Philip and Phyllis Keidel; my parents-in-law, Stephan and Selma Zneimer; my brother, Biff; and brother-in-law, Bill Bierlin; for their ongoing support. Finally and most importantly, my wife, Carole, and kids, Andy and Carly, have truly made this book a family affair. The journey has taken a lot out of all of us. I am confident that it will have been worth the price.

PART 1

Understanding Organizational Design

The Triadic Nature of Organization

"The principles of pattern formation, aggregation,
and transformation seem to be the same in matter and in the
human brain, and if properly formulated they may provide
a kind of visual metaphor that will serve to join and mutually
illuminate physics on the one hand and geological, biological,
and social history on the other—with art in between.
What I seem to have been reaching toward is
not a logical philosophy, not a system of words to be
communicated and refined by discussion, but rather a system
of patterns to be experienced visually and turned into meaning
by the sensual finding of a shared duality of the
external relations with those of the patterns of and on and
in an individual brain."

—CYRIL STANLEY SMITH, *A SEARCH FOR STRUCTURE*

▲ The leader of a multidisciplinary management consulting team on location at a client's site abruptly resigned. He was replaced by the most senior member of the project team. The new leader brought

3

together all the consultants to explain his approach to management: "When you have a team of all-stars, you don't manage them. You just let them play. Well, that's what you guys are. You can manage by yourselves." Several consultants took his comments as license to do their own thing, just as the overall engagement demanded greater collaboration across specialties. The client organization soon became dissatisfied with the consultants' performance and terminated the project.[1]

▲ A high-tech manufacturing company designed and built a one million-square-foot facility that it considered state-of-the-art. This plant was an industrial engineer's masterpiece. Everything was geared to full-bore volume and efficiency: two thousand people's tasks blueprinted to mesh. The facility bombed. The design could tolerate no surprises, which would have been fine if all the plant's products had been standard, off-the-shelf varieties. But few were. Although the major components of most products were standardized, customers typically requested custom features. In short order the new plant became overrun by expediters crisscrossing the floor trying to find jobs and get them completed. And labor relations were dreadful. Workers had absolutely no sense of their individual value in the monolith; they responded rationally by repeatedly going on strike.

The facility was temporarily salvaged by dividing it into several *neighborhoods*—self-contained work clusters designed to give workers a feeling of belonging. But this action proved too little, too late—and eventually the plant was sold (and converted into an exhibition hall).

▲ The director of training for a major industrial corporation was committed to helping move her firm from an authoritarian style of decision-making to one that was more collaborative. She decided that her department should "model" the desired organization-wide process and, accordingly, determined that all future training decisions would be made consensually by her and her staff. This initiative never got off the ground. It soon became clear that certain issues were unresolvable except by fiat. At the same time, other decisions concerned individual matters that had nothing to do with the larger department. The net effect of this short-lived experiment was to sour many people on the very idea of collaboration.

THE PREMISE OF THIS BOOK

Each failure just described actually occurred; each was the consequence of a limited mental model. In the first case, the consulting project director interpreted reality strictly in terms of professional staff elbow room, or *autonomy*. In the second case, corporate planners attempted to "machine" the factory and the workers—to *control* the workplace. In the third case, the training administrator identified with what she had recently learned about "teamwork," which boiled down to *cooperation*. Realistically, professionals' work does call for autonomy, large-scale manufacturing does demand control, and teamwork does depend on cooperation. But each of these situations—like most organizational problems—required that all three variables be taken into account.

The design/change literature commonly attributes failure to employee "resistance" and/or the absence of top-management "commitment." I believe that both these conditions are likely to have cognitive roots. Employee resistance (as in the second example) tends to be a predictable reaction to technocratic managerial thinking that ignores the human realm. And what is often seen as a lack of commitment on the part of senior management is better understood as ample commitment, but to a restricted worldview.

We make decisions based on the way we frame life. We decide—and design—as we think (and feel). In other words, human organization reflects cognitive organization. But more often than not, our cognitive processes fail to match organizational reality. We tend to treat a three-variable world as though it consists of only one or two variables.

In *Leadership and the New Science*, Margaret Wheatley argues that since nature consists essentially of relationships, it stands to reason that human organizations do as well. To take this idea a step further, *organizational design* may be defined as *the purposeful specification of relationships*. Organizations are inherently triadic because there are only three ways in which people can relate, without conflict, to each other— patterns that correspond to the three core design variables identified above: autonomy, control, and cooperation, as depicted in exhibit 1-1:

Exhibit 1-1

TYPES OF HUMAN RELATIONSHIP

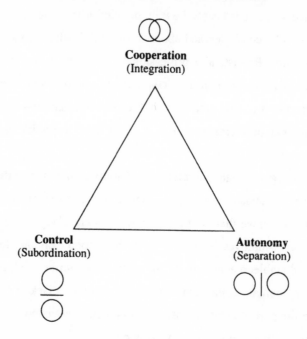

Take any two (or more) individuals—say, Jack and Jill. How can they constructively interact? There are three archetypal ways. Jack and Jill can (1) each do his/her own thing and have minimal contact; (2) settle on a hierarchical (boss/subordinate) arrangement; or (3) collaborate as peers. Now substitute, for Jack and Jill, any two groups, departments, divisions, or corporations. The choices are identical. The design problem is how best to blend these alternatives, which are inherently at odds.[2]

The challenge of balancing conflicting perspectives confronts not only every organization, but every society. Throughout the world, nations are moving from totalitarian to democratic forms of government. As many of these countries have yet to discover—and as established democracies, including the United States, often have to rediscover—successfully managing the transition will require triangulating an informed, self-starting *electorate* (autonomy), a sound *governmental structure* of checks and balances (control), and a *collaborative spirit* on the part of both officials and citizens (cooperation). To the extent that all three requisites are met, then a nation will boast three healthy sectors: private (autonomy), public (control), and voluntary (cooperation).

Unfortunately, too many organizations—as well as societies—fail to consider all of the relevant variables. In a word, they trivialize. Thus, each of the three cases cited at the beginning of this chapter amounts to one-variable management. These patterns appear to be all too common. Business buzzwords of the past two decades exemplify single-variable thinking (or at best, two-variable thinking), with most such labels signifying autonomy *or* control *or* cooperation, as shown in exhibit 1-2.

The overwhelming tendency for management is to become obsessed with control. We continuously encounter the naive impression that organizational design problems can be "fixed" by "installing" new technology. In the same vein, scores of managers are convinced that *design* equals *structure* equals *organization chart*—or, reporting relations—and that changing design amounts to little more than altering boxes and lines. Triangular design differs profoundly from such thinking. The triangular approach does not dismiss organization

7

Exhibit 1-2

CLUSTERS OF BUSINESS BUZZWORDS

	AUTONOMY	CONTROL	COOPERATION
Diversity	x		
Empowerment	x		(x)
Entrepreneurialism	x		
Radical decentralization	x		
Downsizing		x	
Rightsizing		x	
Restructuring		x	
Reengineering	(x)	x	
Quality of worklife	(x)		x
Employee involvement	(x)		x
Teambuilding			x
Multiskilling			x

charts; rather, it recognizes that they are partial, not crucial. As exhibit 3-9 and part 2 (chapters 4–6) make clear, design encompasses several additional dimensions—including character, capabilities, layout, reward systems, and decision systems.

ORGANIZATIONAL DESIGN AS MINDSET

My concept of triangular design began to take shape in 1980, when I was faced with the challenge of conveying complex organizational ideas[3] to a reluctant undergraduate class that included several varsity athletes. I took the usual pedantic approach—beginning with definitions. Yawns. I then used the blackboard to illustrate three different organizational structures—decentralized, centralized, and team-oriented.

More yawns. At that point, in frustration, I turned away from the class and stared at my abstract drawings for maybe five to ten seconds. All of a sudden I saw the patterns of America's major team sports pop out! I then faced the class and asked my athlete-students which pictures matched which games. It was immediately obvious to most of the class (including nonathletes) that what we had before us were representations of baseball, football, and basketball. These metaphors saved the day, and quite possibly the course.

Over the past fourteen years I have had countless comparable, if less dramatic, experiences of "seeing" organizational patterns—especially *triadic* patterns. To me, it has become abundantly clear that a large proportion of organizational issues are a play on autonomy, control, and cooperation. As a consequence, the focus of my work has evolved from *metaphor*, as expressed in my first book *Game Plans*; to *method* in *Corporate Players*; and now to *mindset*.

It is ironic that although approximately one-half of the human brain is dedicated to visual processing, so little of the organizational *design* literature helps managers to "picture" alternative organizational patterns.[4] By contrast, *Seeing Organizational Patterns* provides a system of triangles that capture the major dimensions of design vividly and economically. (Almost all of its images are variations on exhibit 1-1.)

Perhaps the best metaphor for this book is a 1993 compilation of three-dimensional illusions, *Magic Eye: A New Way of Looking at the World*.[5] This work, which generated enormous interest in Japan and then became a best-seller in the United States, consists of a series of color pictures that appear to be standard, two-dimensional renderings. However, if one stares "into" these computer-generated fields, eventually a three-dimensional pattern becomes visible to the naked eye. According to the dust jacket, "Once you discover your MAGIC EYE, a whole new world of experience will open to you. You will be astounded by the depth and clarity of the *totally hidden* image that develops before you like an instant photo!"

Seeing Organizational Patterns provides a remarkably similar conceptual experience. At first glance, any organization is an overwhelming mosaic of people, titles, buildings, machines, materials, and systems. But this surface portrait is like the complex color graphics in *Magic Eye*: It obscures the deeper—and simpler—structure contained within. The real stuff requires a more careful look. Once the triangular pattern has been grasped, it can be applied to all manner of organizational concerns and problems. Design and change therefore become largely a matter of triangulation—identifying parallels with autonomy/control/cooperation and making the appropriate tradeoffs.

Historically in management theory, triangles have been associated with rigid, pyramidal organization structure. My use of this form is a radical departure. For although the triangle symbolizes *stability* (it is the strongest planar figure), it may also symbolize *leverage* (by serving as a fulcrum) and *change* (as represented by *delta*, the fourth letter of the Greek alphabet). Indeed, throughout Western history—from Plato to Frank Lloyd Wright and Buckminster Fuller—the triangle has been appreciated as a generative, universal building shape. It can play the same role in human organizations.

TRIANGULAR DESIGN: AN OVERVIEW

Buckminster Fuller argues that nature has an underlying triangular structure: "Everything that you have ever recognized in [the] Universe as a pattern is re-cognited as the same pattern you have seen before. Because only the triangle persists as a constant pattern, any recognized patterns are inherently recognizable only by virtue of their triangularly structured pattern integrities. Recognition is as dependent on triangulation as is original cognition. Only triangularly structured patterns are regenerative patterns. Triangular structuring is a pattern integrity itself. This is what we mean by *structure*."[6]

Triangular design applies Fuller's perspective to human organization. It reflects Margaret Wheatley's conviction that "If nature uses certain principles to create her infinite diversity, it is highly probable that those principles apply to human organizations."[7] Triangular design thus provides a way to balance—and continuously rebalance—any organization across multiple dimensions, each of which incorporates the autonomy/control/cooperation triad.

Most organizational issues require striking three simultaneous tradeoffs, as indicated in exhibit 1-3.

Exhibit 1-3
ORGANIZATIONAL DESIGN TRADEOFFS

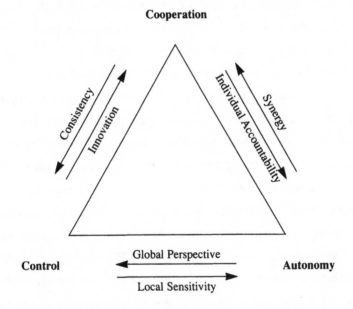

Autonomy versus control is the classic field-versus-headquarters dilemma: nitty gritty versus big picture.[8] Those in the field are "where the rubber meets the road," as the famous tire commercial used to put it. They are in touch with customer needs and geographical nuances in a way that remote corporate managers and staffers can rarely be. What field personnel tend to lack, however, is a view of the whole.

Control versus cooperation is tantamount to consistency versus innovation. McDonald's can assure us that every hamburger will look, taste, smell, and feel the same, whether it is served in New York, New Mexico, or New Zealand. But the price of this guarantee is limited flexibility, both in corporate practices and in employees' behavior. Contrast McDonald's machinelike precision with the dynamics of the group that developed Data General's Eagle computer—the subject of Tracy Kidder's best-seller, *The Soul of a New Machine*: "The entire Eclipse Group, especially its managers, seemed to be operating on instinct. Only the simplest visible arrangements existed among them. They kept no charts and graphs or organizational tables that meant anything. But those webs of voluntary, mutual responsibility, the product of many signings-up, held them together."[9]

Autonomy versus cooperation is equivalent to accountability versus synergy—the individual versus the group. The more an organization stresses individual or unit accountability, the less likely it is to benefit from spontaneous cooperation among individuals or units. Conversely, the greater the commitment to synergy, the more difficult it is to sort out each player's contribution. As Kidder observed in his epilogue, "the building of Eagle really did constitute a collective effort, for now that they had finished, they themselves were having a hard time agreeing on what each individual had contributed."[10]

Exhibit 1-4 presents some universal tradeoffs that loosely parallel autonomy/control/cooperation—in a way that reflects what architectural theorist Christopher Alexander has characterized as "nature's relaxed geometry."[11] Every manager in every organization repeatedly makes choices that involve triads such as those in this list. The difficulty is that too often such choices are made without any awareness that three variables are involved. At best, two-variable thinking patterns prevail.

Exhibit 1-4
SOME UNIVERSAL TRADEOFFS

AUTONOMY	CONTROL	COOPERATION
Environment	Systems	People
Natural/biological	Rational/analytical	Social/cultural
Discovery	Authority	Development
Identity	Method	Purpose
Freedom	Discipline	Sharing
Independence	Dependence	Interdependence
Uniqueness	Continuity	Reciprocity
Surprise/serendipity	Predictability/stability	Change/transition
Positives-increasing	Negatives-decreasing	Different
Product/market	Production/maintenance	Interaction/teamwork
Customer	Shareholder	Employee
Effectiveness	Efficiency	Intention
Differentiation	Cost	Flexibility
Separation	Subordination	Integration
Competition	Conflict	Collaboration
Behavior	Specification	Engagement
Bottom-up	Top-down	Lateral
Player	Coach	Team
Baseball ("Fill out the lineup card")	American football ("Prepare the game plan")	Basketball ("Influence the flow")

Hence, less-than-optimal plans, decisions, and commitments are generated. Such need not be the case.

Consider the effectiveness/efficiency/intention triad (in the middle third of the list). The distinction between the first two elements of this set is familiar: Efficiency is "doing things right"; effectiveness is "doing the right things." The usual point of this contrast is to emphasize the primacy of effectiveness. If one is going in the wrong direction (i.e., ineffective), then it is actually dysfunctional to be efficient. But there is a third variable that tends to be left out—intention. Effectiveness (the *what*) and efficiency (the *how*) are never enough; a direction should be taken for the right reason—one that is meaningful (the *why*).

Countless organizational change programs have floundered because (1) they were undertaken for no clear reason; (2) they were undertaken for the wrong reason (that is, wrong or invalid in most people's eyes); or (3) over time, they lost their connection with reason. Ignoring or discounting intention—the *why*—can be expensive. But so can ignoring or discounting any other variable within the autonomy/control/cooperation framework. Chapter 2 systematically maps varieties of design failure in terms of this triad.

Varieties of Design Failure

"A major issue that is getting practically
no attention in the management literature is the reality
that in many cases the chief executive officer does not have the
conceptual capacity to grasp the degree of complexity that
he or she must now confront. In short, they simply do not know
what they are really up against and what is happening to them
and to their organizations, let alone knowing what to do about it.
They simply cannot absorb the range of information they
should and organize it from its multiple sources and focus it
on the organizations' problems in a way that would both
become vision and strategy."

—HARRY LEVINSON, "WHY THE BEHEMOTHS FELL,"
AMERICAN PSYCHOLOGIST, MAY 1994

Without question, cognitively challenged individuals can be found at
senior levels (and all other levels) of virtually every major corporation.
But there is a larger issue than native intellect and selection/place-
ment/promotion. Managers, professionals, and others throughout today's

organizations—regardless of their intelligence quotients—desperately need user-friendly ways to organize complexity without trivializing it. I believe that the concepts laid out in this book can help to make sense of apparent chaos *and* are widely learnable[1]—especially since these concepts are represented graphically. *Organizational* IQ can be developed.

THREE WAYS TO FAIL

Managers and organizations can fail in any of three general ways:[2]

▲ By *over*doing their top priority—whether it be autonomy *or* control *or* cooperation.

▲ By *under*doing their bottom priority.

▲ By operating *without* priorities.

These flawed patterns are indicated by the shaded areas in exhibit 2-1, a graphic that one client described as a "triangular doughnut."

Exhibit 2-1
THREE WAYS TO FAIL

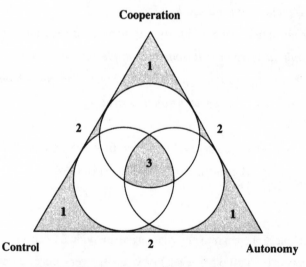

1: Overdo top priority (one-variable design)
2: Underdo bottom priority (two-variable design)
3: Operate without priorities (undifferentiated design)

ONE-VARIABLE DESIGN

One-variable managers (and organizations) live in a world of black-*or*-white (or, more generally, black or non-black). Such individuals are zealots. They are true believers who often unwittingly try to impose their worldview on everyone else. They have a mental hammer; therefore, everything (and sometimes everyone) gets hammered. Any of the three organizational variables may be exaggerated.

Overdoing Autonomy. In this pattern, the part takes precedence over the whole. Players—whether individuals or units—tend to manipulate the larger organization to their advantage, with scant concern for reciprocity. The operative motto is "Everyone for him (her) self." Many companies' fullbore pursuit of decentralization has resulted in their overemphasizing autonomy. Ray Stata, chairman of Analog Devices, admitted that in rethinking his firm's organizational design, "It became clear to all of us that our almost fanatical commitment to decentralization was impeding progress."[3] In another highly-decentralized company that had grown rapidly by acquisition, a corporate technical specialist became branded as "dangerous" because of his (sensible) contention that greater hierarchical discipline (control) and electronic networking (cooperation) were in that organization's best interests. Within a few years, this individual's career path was blocked and he resigned; and the company struggled financially, as its disparate and far-flung operating units continued to go their own ways.

Conglomerates are especially prone to the autonomy-seeking tendencies of their parts—a condition only made worse by excessive portfolio diversity. In general, when conglomeration devolves into agglomeration, the market value of an organization's parts may well exceed that of the whole. Investment bankers instinctively grasp this math and use it to recommend busting up a corporation that has become a hodgepodge.

At any system level, the tendency to overemphasize autonomy may

stem in part from swallowing the notion of personal liberty and freedom, without a concomitant sense of responsibility and community. A
1992 *Economist* article conveys lament in its title and subtitle:
"America's vigilante values: freedom of action under the law can
sometimes go too far."[4] Or take the title and inset of another 1992 article, this one by Richard Reeves in the *Philadelphia Inquirer*: "In Los
Angeles, diversity in the schools is being taken to its logical end—
chaos: the excitement of having a child in Los Angeles public schools
is waking up each morning and wondering if they will be open."[5]

A frightening example of excessive autonomy may be the remains
of the Soviet Union—no small irony given the fact that the old USSR
was a classically over-controlled society, with all the decisions made
at the top of the empire. Since that nation's breakup, however, the
world may have become even more precarious, as the various pieces
continuously vie for power. (Former Soviet foreign minister Eduard A.
Shevardnadze has been quoted as saying that the West should feel "ter-
rorized" by the nuclear threat posed by the USSR's dissolution.[6])

Overdoing Control. The philosophical basis for much corporate
control is Frederick W. Taylor's concept of "scientific management":
a few brains at the top, a phalanx of brawn at the bottom. Today, the
spirit of Taylorism is exemplified by a popular—if vacuous—management exhortation: "Lead, follow, or get out of the way!" In other
words, either give orders or take orders—or begone! Individual contribution and nonhierarchical cooperation have little value.

The litany of organizations that continue to overdo control is enormous. It ranges from "old style" manufacturers in all industries to public sector bureaucracies such as the U.S. Postal Service—with its sorry
history of burdensome regulations, adversarial relationships, and physical violence. I experienced control-freak management directly in the
early 1970s, as a first-time "analyst" with a management consulting
firm specializing in industrial engineering. The job involved measur-

ing indirect labor/supervisory work and recommending payroll cuts. The only concern was chopping costs. Everything else—craftsmanship/quality, service/flexibility, teamwork/learning—was irrelevant. This work virtually demanded one-variable thinking.

Perhaps the most depressing episode of my short tenure with this firm came during the preparation of a labor savings presentation for a large industrial client. One of the client managers who was assisting us had developed an imaginative approach to documenting expected savings: He systematically proved three different ways of calculating client benefits. No sooner had this individual outlined his approach to our project manager than the latter humiliated him in front of several of his peers. The charge: that showing alternate methods for arriving at savings betrayed indecisiveness. There could be one way, and one way only!

The joke among a few of us short-timers was that if you inserted a true-blue efficiency expert into a company that had just been measured and tightened to the gills, he would proceed to do the whole cost-reduction program all over again—step by insipid step. Is this mindset ancient history? Unfortunately, no. The relentless hacking away at "head count" by one corporate giant after another seems like "déjà vu all over again," to quote Yogi Berra.

Overdoing Cooperation. This is the least common of the three one-variable categories, but it does happen. Perhaps the past decade's most publicized case of overdoing cooperation was the demise of People Express Airlines—a failure that can be characterized as trying to run a big airline the same way you used to run a small airline. As another chief executive remarked about People CEO Donald Burr in early 1985, long before that carrier's troubles had become front-page news, "He's passed a point of critical mass. There's a point where structure counts."[7]

In the early 1990s, Compaq Computer Corp.'s extreme commit-

19

ment to collaboration may have cost CEO Rod Canion his job, while across the Pacific, Honda Motor Co. revised its highly consensual decision-making process—which historically had featured wide-ranging, informal discussions known as *waigaya*—to incorporate more hierarchical discipline. Compaq's and Honda's problems were similar to that experienced at People Express: Both companies had outgrown their ability to rely on informal patterns of authority.

Sometimes "teambuilders"—consultants who make a living by helping people work together constructively—are unwitting examples of encouraging inordinate cooperation, for one reason: They simply do not understand organizational design. The tipoff? When asked about organizational design or structure, they immediately dismiss the subject as "just a bunch of boxes and lines." Conventional teambuilding is concerned with "soft" small-group dynamics and interpersonal relations: two-way communications, giving and receiving feedback, role clarification, establishing norms of trust, collaborative problem-solving. Rarely do teambuilders grapple seriously with such "hard" organizational realms as reporting relations, authority structures, and reward systems.

When teambuilders do venture into structures and systems, it is often naively. Many self-styled "process consultants" continue to encourage organizational "teams" to reach virtually *every* decision in a collaborative manner. Such an ambition is unrealizable. In any social system, some decisions will always have to be mandated, while others will have to be delegated to specific individuals. (The range of decision-making patterns, and the conditions that favor each, are considered at length in chapter 6.)

Consultants are not always to blame when a group "cooperates" to excess. In one major industrial plant, a facilitator was brought in to help the top-management contingent "become a cohesive team with a common purpose." The problem was, this "team" encompassed seventeen people. The facilitator suggested that the group either be reduced in size or be broken into two teams. Several individuals rejected these ideas because they feared that they personally would lose visibility, and therefore power, if they were excluded altogether or wound up on the team that did not include the top manager. The facilitator's response: try to meet and interact consensually—for the most part—as a group of seventeen; then, if and when the process becomes laborious, consider other options. The whole group met—a day offsite every six weeks—for over a year before their frustrations became intolerable. At that point, everyone agreed to split into two smaller teams—a planning team (concerned with relations external to the plant) and an operating team (whose focus was production), with two or three overlapping members. (The new arrangement worked like a charm.)

TWO-VARIABLE DESIGN

Two-variable thinkers come in two varieties: (1) those who seek a compromise or tradeoff between two variables, and (2) those who try to combine or maximize two variables. The former believe that increasing one variable necessarily decreases the other; they live in a shades-of-gray world. The latter are convinced that both variables can be maximized without having to trade off anything; they live in a world of black-*and*-white.

Underdoing Autonomy. During the past two decades in the United States, much of what has passed for quality of worklife, employee involvement, and Japanese management techniques has attempted to counterbalance control with cooperation, but with virtually no attention to autonomy. The individual in such schemes has not been considered independently of his or her role as a group member. Indeed, at least through the 1970s, the mainstream management literature all but excluded non-bureaucratic, non-manufacturing types of organizations—most notably, professional service firms—in which individuals, not groups or departments, are often the key players.

A similar omission can be found in the conduct—and analysis—of many family businesses. It is only in the last fifteen years that management scholars have begun to pay serious attention to this class of organization. Such attention has focused on conceptualizing the business system (whose survival/growth needs correspond chiefly to control) and the family system (which is closer to cooperation) as overlapping circles, with each recognized as having legitimate needs and claims. But lost in this neat, two-ring portrait are the concerns and aspirations of individual family members—especially those who are wedded to neither the business nor the family.

Underdoing Control.[8] There may be no more blatant example of this pattern than the profligate deregulation of the 1980s—the effects of which ranged from massive real estate failures to the savings and loan debacle. As high-profile as the latter patterns are, there is a lower-profile tendency that also gives cause for concern. In the management literature, it has become fashionable to talk about *nonhierarchical* and *boundaryless* organizations. Although efforts to minimize hierarchy and needless boundaries are salutary, this thrust can be taken too far. No society, organization, or family can ever function without some measure of hierarchical control, role specialization, and sense of limits—any more than a computer network such as Internet can ever be totally open, with no need for participating firms to erect "firewalls" in order to safeguard proprietary information.[9] Although it is highly probable that tomorrow's leading-edge corporations will need to exercise less top-down control—and encourage commensurately more autonomy and cooperation (the subject of chapter 8)—it is naive to think that the need for hierarchy will disappear.

Underdoing Cooperation. Most corporate managers that I have observed perceive organizational design as linear—reducible to a continuum of centralization (control) at one end and decentralization (autonomy) at the other, with teamwork (cooperation) nowhere in sight. The firm, like a trolley, goes back and forth between the two extremes: "Things have become too bureaucratic; we need to drive decision-making down to those who are where the action is"; or "Things have gotten out of hand; we need to concentrate authority where we have the big picture."

If there is a "typical" corporate manager, chances are this individual is committed to societal autonomy (minimal external constraints on exercising power) and organizational control (minimal internal constraints). Cooperation hardly enters the equation in either sphere. In general, collaboration has not figured prominently in Western thinking. According to Michael Schrage,

> The Western tradition of intellectual thought doesn't embrace collaboration as a vital creative behavior. You don't find collaboration as part of Aristotelian or Platonic thought (which is ironic, given the role of dialogue in creating enlightenment). Nor is collaboration a part of the Judeo-Christian ethic of community. Adam Smith talked about the "division of labor," not collaboration, Marx heralded the "labor theory of value," yet left the collaborative processes that yield this value virtually unexamined.
>
> Similarly, the nascent sciences of human thought and behavior give collaboration short shrift. Pavlov, John B. Watson, B.F. Skinner, and the behaviorist school scarcely touch collaboration as a social process. Freud brilliantly explored and described the inner beyonds of the human psyche, but not in the context of the way people create shared understandings.[10]

Jeffrey Pfeffer finds a similar omission in the field of managerial training, much of which rests on noncooperative economics concepts (such as agency theory and transaction cost theory). He notes that economists, as a group, tend to be less cooperative than non-economists: "It is scarcely surprising that training that stresses self-interested behavior, rampant opportunism, and conflicts of interest would produce less collaborative behavior on the part of those exposed to the training and the language used to express these ideas."[11]

The risk with all dyadic thinking is that at least one-third of organizational reality will be ignored.[12] In fact, an optimistic premise underpins some two-variable thinking: the concept of dialectic. From polar positions of thesis and antithesis, a transcendent synthesis will presumably emerge. This logic, however, does not necessarily hold. Whenever a human system or process is grounded in only two variables, four outcomes are possible, but three of these are unfortunate: (1) gridlock or stalemate; (2) an unimaginative compromise to which no one is really committed; and (3) a single-variable solution that results from one side's mugging the other.[13]

In earlier times—when competition, complexity, and change were less severe—two-variable (and even one-variable) thinking was often sufficient. No more. Tomorrow's arena will increasingly belong to managers who are able to balance autonomy, control, and cooperation,[14] with balance implying differentiation as well as integration.

UNDIFFERENTIATED DESIGN

Effective three-variable thinking does not mean maximizing all three variables. Rather, it means emphasizing one or two variables, without neglecting any. An organization that tries to maximize all three patterns will likely lose any sense of priorities. Thus, the senior management team of a major company with which I am familiar prepared a draft vision statement that would have committed the organization equally to individual creativity and risk-taking (autonomy), firm direction and efficiency (control), and flexibility and innovation (cooperation). (Fortunately, these managers came to recognize the confusion in their message and focused their priorities before sharing their ideas with the rest of the firm.)

A widespread example of undifferentiated design is the matrix or two-boss organization (discussed at greater length in chapter 3). Matrix designs implicitly try to achieve the best of all three worlds; consequently, they run a significant risk of realizing none. When an organization tries to be all things to all people all of the time, it usually winds up being nothing to anyone at anytime. If everything is a number-one priority, then nothing is. Unfortunately, the pressures of the late '80s and now the '90s have driven many firms to go for the best of several worlds. Thus we find organizations that feature a new theme or slogan every year or quarter—or even month. One can predict that the greater the number of themes out there, the more they represent divergent organizational pulls, and the faster they turn over, the more cynical organizational members will become.[15] In one company, a prolonged salvo of new "strategic thrusts" (which covered the autonomy/control/cooperation gamut) was likened to what used to be called the "bum of the month" practice in boxing—that is, scheduling a succession of patsies in order to inflate a contender's record. Needless to say, not one of these initiatives was taken seriously.

Many instances of undifferentiated design represent an attempt to consider simultaneously four or more variables (some of which may correspond to autonomy, control, and/or cooperation)—a pattern that might be called *polygonal* thinking. (A polygon is a closed planar figure, typically with four or more sides and angles.) The problem is that few people can process and prioritize this degree of complexity. Corporate planner Peter Schwartz explains why he favors triads when constructing future scenarios: ". . . people's minds can cope with only two or three possibilities. Two may not capture reality, so you often use three. On rare occasions you might consider four. Any more choices will produce a hopeless muddle."[16]

In chapter 1, I argued that business buzzwords exemplify one-variable thinking, and then I matched representative jargon with autonomy, control, and cooperation, respectively. One-variable thinkers and undifferentiated thinkers have essentially the same problem, even if their responses differ: Both are unable to organize complexity. The former try to escape by trivializing, while the latter stay put and become engulfed.

Whereas one- and two-variable thinkers see the world in black/white/shades of gray, triangular thinkers view the world *in color*. In fact, the idea of triangular design evokes a device from physics called the Maxwell color triangle—an equilateral triangle whose vertices are the primary colors of light (not pigments): blue, red, and green. Virtually any color in the spectrum can be located within this shape.[17]

The remainder of this book elaborates triangular thinking and organization, and shows that triangular design can clarify the essential structure of a host of organizational issues. Successive chapters:

▲ Describe several practical applications of triangular design (chapter 3),

▲ Present an idealized diagnostic profile (chapters 4 through 6),

▲ Provide conceptual and metaphorical perspectives for understanding triangular design (chapters 7 and 8).

Triangulating Autonomy, Control, and Cooperation

"In the end, running a company in a borderless world is about trying to resolve a number of apparent contradictions. Firms have to be responsive to national needs [autonomy], yet seek to exploit knowhow on a worldwide basis [cooperation], while, all the time, striving to produce and distribute goods globally as efficiently as possible [control]. Many companies manage to achieve one, maybe even two, of these objectives. It is hard to think of any company that has yet managed to balance all three simultaneously."

—"THE DISCREET CHARM OF THE MULTICULTURAL MULTINATIONAL,"
THE ECONOMIST, JULY 30, 1994

The challenge is threefold. Every organization, and unit within it, must (1) *prioritize* autonomy, control, and cooperation so that necessary tradeoffs are made; (2) *integrate* these variables because all three are essential and interdependent; and (3) *focus* on whichever variable(s) require attention at any given time, regardless of their priority.

Chapter 2 concentrated on the "gray" areas of the Organizational Design Triangle—examples of imbalance, or patterns that are prone to failure. This chapter is concerned primarily with the white areas—workable combinations. Most corporate designs can be expressed in familiar business language within the triangle, as shown in exhibit 3-1.

Exhibit 3-1

GENERIC ORGANIZATIONAL DESIGNS

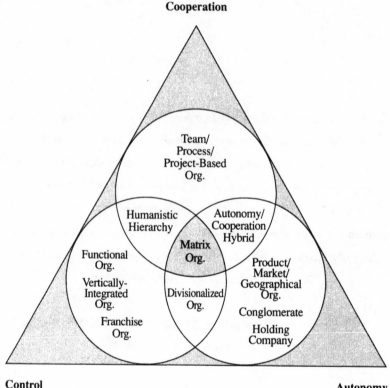

Autonomy-based designs—whether organized around product, market, region, customer type, financial criterion, or some other basis—feature relatively freestanding units. Control-based designs are exemplified by (1) the classic functional bureaucracy, with a single research and development

(R&D) department, manufacturing/operations department, and sales/marketing activity—for all products; (2) vertical integration—the meshing of a chain of economic activities, from resource acquisition through processing, distribution, sales, and, perhaps, post-sale service; and (3) franchise organizations—to the extent that units' behavior is programmed. Cooperation-based designs include (1) self-managing, multifunctional work groups ("autonomous" or semi-autonomous teams); (2) horizontal designs centered on business processes (such as information management and new-product development);[1] and (3) ad hoc, project-based task forces drawn from various disciplines, locations, and organizational levels.

Divisionalized organizations tend to be more or less symmetrical blends of autonomy and control, with minimal cooperation evident among operating units. The *humanistic hierarchy* describes various attempts to democratize inherently rigid, high-control designs—often through quality-of-worklife or employee-involvement/empowerment overlays. The *autonomy/cooperation hybrid* signals an organizational pattern that is treated at length in chapter 8.

Note that matrix organization is depicted as stuck in the middle of the triangle. Matrix designs typically try to combine an input (control) bias and an output (autonomy) bias by requiring certain managers to report to both an input (for example, functional) boss and an output (product/market) boss. But to make this combination work, considerable voluntary cooperation among all parties is essential; without question, the absence of such cooperation has sunk many a matrix. Yet when cooperation *is* forthcoming, the priorities among autonomy, control, and cooperation are likely to become muddled. What we have here is an essentially no-win design, reminiscent of the worst properties of a helicopter—which has been described as a machine whose every part seems to be trying to pull everything apart.

There are, to be sure, successful examples of matrix organization, and dual-reporting relationships can work so long as autonomy, control, and cooperation are carefully prioritized. Still, maintaining a matrix is one tough balancing act—especially for very long. This pattern may be most effective as a "switch" or bridge between more robust designs.

ORGANIZATION-WIDE PLANNING AND DESIGN

James River Graphics (hereafter, "Graphics") illustrates the use of the triangular methodology as a diagnostic and planning framework. Graphics' managers used the triangle over an extended time period to assess historical and current designs and to specify desired futures.

Graphics was part of Richmond-based James River Corporation from 1978 until 1991 (when it was sold to an investment group). I consulted with Graphics from 1983 through 1988. At the end of this period, Graphics was made up of seven divisions, with the collective charter "to provide specialty coated products of *superior value* to customers primarily in the information materials and decorative products markets." From 1978 through 1988, Graphics evolved through a series of transitions, as depicted in exhibit 3-2.[2]

Exhibit 3-2
MULTIPLE TRANSITIONS AT JAMES RIVER GRAPHICS

Cooperation

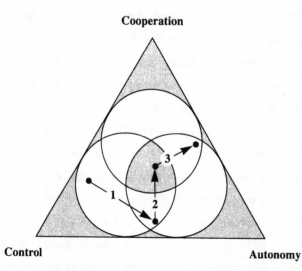

Control

Autonomy

1: Acquisition to divisionalization (1978-81)
2: Divisionalization to matrix (1984-85)
3: Matrix to autonomy/cooperation hybrid (1985-88)

Transition One. James River acquired the Graphics operation from another major paper company in 1978. At that time, Graphics was functionally organized—centrally controlled, top-heavy, and layered. James River streamlined the organization by eliminating a considerable number of middle-management positions. As the complexity facing the firm increased over the next three years, however, it became clear that a functional design, no matter how efficiently staffed, was not up to the task. Top functional managers were being spread too thin across an ever-expanding array of products, markets, and technologies. Accordingly, in 1981, Graphics split into two divisions, reflecting its two major product categories. The transition was from a control bias to an even blend of control and autonomy.

Transition Two. When I first began consulting with Graphics in 1983, the firm was still divisionalized but was experiencing a number of organizational blockages. Divisional agendas often conflicted because, though separate, the units shared resources. Resolving disputes about such things as machine availability and maintenance priorities required a cumbersome process of hierarchical referral. Graphics' senior management believed that a more team-oriented style was needed. In design terms, this meant greater cooperation relative to both control (the prevailing mode for vertical relationships) and autonomy (the prevailing mode for horizontal relationships).

The senior team resolved to increase cooperation throughout Graphics by taking several related steps. First, they articulated a mission and a set of guiding behavioral principles. Second, the senior team took part in a team-building process and then authorized similar training for the rest of the organization. Third, the team reconstituted itself as Graphics' "Management Operating Committee" (MOC), thereby recognizing its *collective* responsibility for managing the entire enterprise. Fourth, the top team reorganized the firm into a modified matrix in order to maximize communication across boundaries. To support the new structure, Graphics' senior team developed a *decision* matrix that laid out authorities within the MOC and between this group and the company as a whole; this document then became integrated

31

into the basic teambuilding menu and was spread down and across the entire organization.

Transition Three. Between 1985 and 1988, Graphics acquired five new divisions. Whereas the organization had been concentrated in a single (New England) location, Graphics now became spread across several locations—ranging from the west coast of the United States to the United Kingdom. Given the likelihood of continued growth and increasing diversity, it seemed probable in late 1988 that centralized control would diminish even further as a management control mechanism. As President Karl V. Kraske told his team at the time, "It is not my job to run your businesses, and I have no intention of 'orchestrating' anything. My role is to help identify and exploit overlaps between the businesses, to balance competing needs, and to remove artificial barriers that separate us."

At year's end, Kraske and his divisional vice presidents were actively shaping the organization into an autonomy/cooperation hybrid that would blend division independence and interdependence without sacrificing necessary central controls. More specifically, they were redesigning such organizational dimensions as the decision system (how much authority should division heads have, individually and as a group?), information flow (how extensively should each division's technical abilities and production capacities be shared?), and reward system (what balance should the profit-sharing formula strike between divisional performance and group performance?).

Graphics' composition, management, and (eventually) ownership changed after 1988—and I no longer consulted with the organization. Nonetheless, Graphics' use of the triangular methodology over a several-year time frame—during which the firm both grew and diversified—remains exemplary. That framework made it possible (1) to chart continuously the future in light of the present and the past; and (2) to go back and forth between general perspectives (using the triangle as a compass) and concrete actions (revising reporting relationships, the decision system, the reward system, and so on).

FUNCTIONAL PLANNING AND DESIGN

In their classic book, *Organization and Environment*, Paul Lawrence and Jay Lorsch define *differentiation* as "the difference in cognitive and emotional orientation among managers in different functional departments."[3] While it is possible to pattern not only whole organizations but whole industries and societies as a balance of autonomy, control, and cooperation, no two parts of the same organization will ever be identical. In my experience, different organizational functions—and functional mindsets—typically correspond to one of three "solution spaces" centered on a particular variable—as shown in exhibit 3-3.

Exhibit 3-3

THREE SOLUTION SPACES

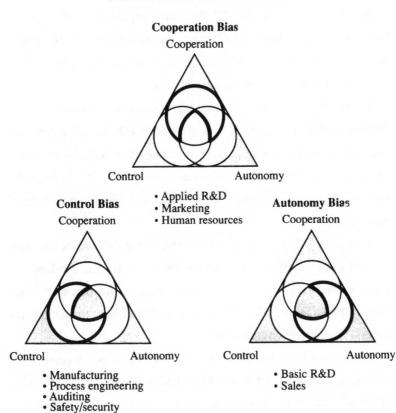

Cooperation Bias
Cooperation

Control   Autonomy

• Applied R&D
• Marketing
• Human resources

Control Bias
Cooperation

Control   Autonomy

• Manufacturing
• Process engineering
• Auditing
• Safety/security

Autonomy Bias
Cooperation

Control   Autonomy

• Basic R&D
• Sales

A solution space is the geometric equivalent of an algebraic "solution set." Given the simple equation, $x + y = 5$, and assuming that both x and y are positive integers, the following solution set solves this equation:

$$x = 1, \qquad y = 4$$
$$x = 2, \qquad y = 3$$
$$x = 3, \qquad y = 2$$
$$x = 4, \qquad y = 1$$

A solution set or space defines the boundaries within which a solution is possible; it provides constrained choice. And although the current vogue is to move away from functional orientations (popularly derided as chimneys or silos or stovepipes) and toward composite business processes (such as customer acquisition and order fulfillment), the realities are that (1) functional organization will always have its time and place, and (2) functional biases must be taken into account whenever an organization attempts to blend disparate functional capabilities into a process-based design.

I have yet to encounter the sales organization that does not have an autonomy bias. The same is true of basic R&D. As defined by the National Science Foundation, *basic research* refers to "original investigations for the advancement of scientific knowledge not having specific commercial objectives."[4] Such work may have a time horizon of thirty years.

Both basic R&D and sales are the habitat of individualists who tend to choose such work in large part for the autonomy that it offers. Yet organizations have ample opportunity to combine this bias with either control (for example, scientific freedom within highly structured parameters) or cooperation (team selling).

Applied R&D, or product commercialization, reflects a cooperation bias that cuts across functional and hierarchical boundaries. So, typically, does marketing, to the extent that it resembles the work of a "middleman"[5] between customer needs and organizational capabilities. In every instance, however, the organization has considerable discretion in integrating this cooperative tendency with either autonomy or control.

Safety and security functions, as well as those related to internal auditing, understandably are biased toward control. Yet there remain opportunities to encourage greater cooperation or autonomy within a control frame. A few years ago, I conducted a seminar for mangers of a company that built nuclear power plants. One participant made the point early on that "We can't do wildly experimental things like, say, an Apple Computer or a Turner Broadcasting can." But she quickly added, "Still, we could be a whole lot less bureaucratic—and much more cooperative—in the way we operate."

Also biased toward control are manufacturing and process engineering, because of their inherent demands for up-front system design/scoping. In fact, it was two major consulting projects—involving manufacturing and engineering, respectively—that gave rise to the use of solution spaces within the triangular framework. In the late 1980s, a *Fortune* 100 industrial client decided to use the triangular scheme to characterize successful Japanese manufacturers. My client sent several groups of its own managers (worldwide) to Japan in order to study exemplary Japanese operating principles and practices. As part of this experience, Japanese managers and professionals were asked to describe their organizations as a balance of autonomy, control, and cooperation. The eight Japanese firms that took part flocked to one part of the triangle, about midway between control and cooperation. My client dubbed this location the *sweet spot* for effective manufacturing—with the term "sweet spot" referring to that part of a golf club head, baseball bat, or tennis racquet (and so on) where, simultaneously, the player achieves maximum power and has a "sweet feel." The resulting graphic (exhibit 3-4) became a valuable tool for communication and discussion across several levels of management.

Exhibit 3-4
MANUFACTURING SWEET SPOT

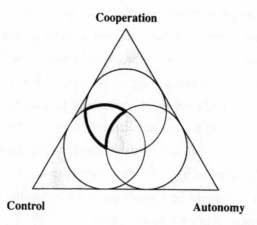

Also in the late 1980s, James River Corporation embarked on an organization-wide analysis of process engineering. This study, under the leadership of vice-president Benjamin A. Thorp, benchmarked nine other capital-intensive North American companies that were noted for their competence in process engineering. We found that these firms clustered in three sections of the control-bias figure (exhibit 3-5).

Exhibit 3-5
PROCESS ENGINEERING ORGANIZATIONAL OPTIONS

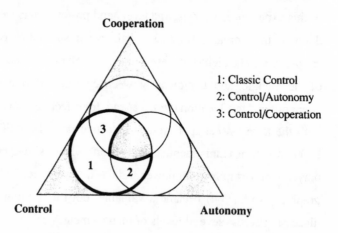

(In the *classic control* pattern, almost all "detail design" work [that is, line drawings] is carried out internally, by engineers from a single corporate department, with direct responsibility to engineering, not manufacturing. In *control/autonomy*, engineering is centralized, but almost all detail design is contracted out to consultants by the manufacturing plants, which have the opportunity to use whatever firm they wish. In *control/cooperation*, considerable detail design is performed in-house, but there is an emphasis on voluntarily sharing engineering resources across regions and/or business units.)

After mapping these engineering organizational designs, we then linked each pattern to a larger corporate type. We found that classic control best suits highly unified companies that tend to have only nominal product/process diversity. Control/autonomy fits firms that are far more diffuse, where corporate performance is roughly the sum of many profit centers' performances. Control/cooperation makes sense for corporations that fall outside the bureaucracy-to-holding-company continuum because they depend on spontaneous cooperation among their various parts.

In parallel, we spelled out aspects of the desired pattern for James River—which we then summarized graphically (exhibit 3-6). Since this study was completed, the company has taken considerable strides toward the desired pattern. Exhibits 3-5 and 3-6 (along with more extensive materials) have also been shared with several other process-intensive corporations (some of which represent different industries) interested in understanding alternative organizational logics.

RETHINKING HUMAN RESOURCES PRIORITIES

An all-time favorite corporate cliche is that "people are our most important asset." To the extent that these words have life, then human resources management (HRM) should exist primarily to support the development of people within the context of organizational needs. Such is often not the case, however, in part because HRM has failed to

37

Exhibit 3-6

DESIRED SPECIFICATIONS FOR PROCESS ENGINEERING AT JAMES RIVER CORPORATION

- Distributed nodes of technical excellence
- Greater interface with/impact on suppliers
- Cumulative learning
- Synergy/flexibility/technology transfer
- Real-time communications throughout the company

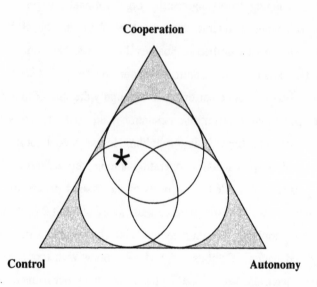

- Technical state-of-the-art
- Global perspective
- Efficiency
- Consistency
- Critical mass of skills
- Protection of proprietary information
- Protection against design changes and cost creep

- Mill/plant ownership of projects
- Local responsiveness and client-identification

think systematically through its functions, roles, and priorities.

The triangular framework has proven useful in conceptualizing organizational alternatives for HRM departments. What follows is a composite of my work with human resources professionals in several very different companies.

HRM consists essentially of three activities: client-responsiveness, system-maintenance, and development. *Client-responsiveness* means reacting to problems or concerns raised by individuals ("clients") from within and outside the organization. Such problems tend to be nonroutine and largely unpredictable; hence, this HRM activity corresponds to *autonomy*.

System-maintenance is the most programmable of the three activities. It consists of carrying out and monitoring ongoing operations such as staffing, appraisal, compensation, career development, and management succession—not to mention complying with various governmental regulations. System-maintenance is rooted in *control*.

Development has to do with increasing individual, group, and organizational capabilities. Developmental initiatives are qualitatively different from the routine concerns of system maintenance. And unlike the client-responsiveness function, development is initiated either within HRM or jointly with particular clients. Development most closely matches *cooperation*.

All three activities are essential. The key issue is prioritization: To what extent is a given organization (or department or individual) biased in a particular direction? Many HRM units are dominated by system-maintenance concerns. Such a pattern may be highly efficient, but it is likely to limit an organization's potential for learning and change. One way to alter this bias is to quantify actual and desired distributions of staff time, and then "explode" the development function into specific roles that change agents should play in the desired organization: consultant, trainer, and facilitator. Exhibit 3-7 displays the

Exhibit 3-7

HRM FUNCTIONS & DEVELOPMENTAL ROLES

Facilitator

Developmental
(Change-Agent)
Roles

Trainer   Consultant

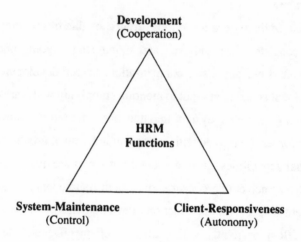

Development
(Cooperation)

HRM
Functions

System-Maintenance   Client-Responsiveness
(Control)   (Autonomy)

triangular set and subset.

The role of *consultant* is the least structured of the three. An individual must be able to range widely throughout the organization. She or he must be able to comprehend complex problems from varied perspectives, as well as demonstrate credibility with people at different organizational levels and units. Consultants tend to work on their own much of the time, and many of their key interactions are one-to-one. This activity parallels *autonomy*.

The role of *trainer*—especially, stand-up trainer—is the most structured. It consists of delivering off-the-shelf packages to relatively passive audiences. Of course, not all training is of this variety; some forms are highly complex and interactive, and demand uncommon pedagogical skills. Still, the role of "basic trainer" in most corporate settings is fairly cut and dried; it is essentially a *control* function.[6]

The role of *facilitator* involves helping small groups or teams to function more effectively. The process of facilitation is less structured than training, but more structured than consulting. Initiative rests with the group, and the facilitator is expected to intervene chiefly on an exception basis. Successful facilitation requires the ability to "feel" the rhythm or tempo of a group's progress, and to improvise from time to time. Facilitation is closer to *cooperation* than to either autonomy or control.

The distinctions among these contrasting developmental roles have provided HR managers with (1) a diagnostic framework for identifying skill shortages and surpluses; and (2) a career-development guide for encouraging either specialization within a role or the development of generalist change-agent skills.

STRUCTURING DIALOGUE

Terry Winograd and Fernando Flores, in *Understanding Computers and Cognition*, argue persuasively that language and conversation are the essence of human organization.[7] Alan Webber echoes this notion: "If the new work of the company is conversation, then what is the job of the manager? Put simply: to create an environment where employees can have productive conversations rather than counterproductive ones, useful conversations rather than useless ones."[8]

The triangular methodology can make a difference. Exhibit 3-8 presents a condensed example of a cluster of triads developed during a preliminary planning session with a client from a major pharmaceutical company. The language below describes words (and lines) I scrib-

Exhibit 3-8

A REPRESENTATIVE STRING OF TRIANGLES
(From consulting with a pharmaceutical company)

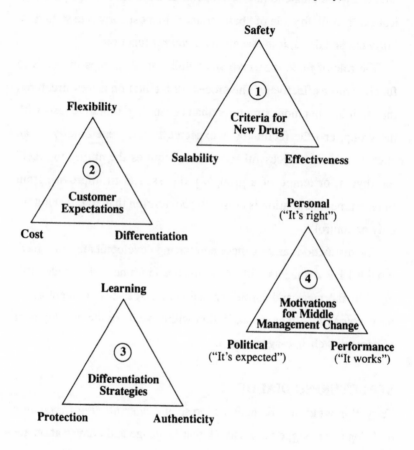

bled on my yellow note pad. Even though the parallels with autonomy, control, and cooperation are loose, this underlying structure helped to pattern our discussion.

Our conversation started with the acknowledgment that an ethical pharmaceutical must be three things: safe, effective, and salable. Safety and effectiveness are primary. The issue of a drug's potential salability and profitability is (or at least should be) subordinate to that of balancing its relative safety (risk) and potential effectiveness (benefit).

We subsequently considered competitive criteria that make a drug salable—viz., differentiation, cost, and flexibility (as defined in chapter 4). Our discussion led to a new triad, *differentiation strategies*. We determined that there are three generic ways that an organization can reinforce differentiation. The first of these is to underscore authenticity—the fact that one's concept or product was the first, the original. Public relations and advertising can be effective in this regard. The second method is to seek protection—in particular, legal support—in the event that someone else tries to appropriate proprietary knowledge, information, and so on. And the third way to reinforce differentiation is through learning—that is, remaining at the cutting edge of a particular subject. One practical result of this discussion was a deeper appreciation of the value of continuous learning.

We then talked about *social* learning and linked this process to participative organizational change. Our attention turned to middle-level managers, who often prove to be less than enthusiastic about finding a different way. At this point, I introduced a triad that had been useful in several other contexts: motivations for middle-management change. I suggested that, initially, skeptical managers are likely to go along with change (to the extent that they do so at all) primarily for political reasons—because such behavior "is expected" by their boss (and pay and promotional opportunities may hang in the balance). After having come on board for political reasons, such individuals may later support organizational change initiatives for performance reasons—because they have seen successful examples and now believe that "it works." The third stage is to embrace cooperative change for personal reasons—because it "is right." The mistake that a lot of senior managers make is unrealistically to expect early commitment by their subordinate managers for personal reasons. It is often sensible to start with political/performance postures and then encourage the humanistic aspect of change motivation to develop over time.

This consulting session generated several additional triads, most of which could be related more or less to autonomy/control/cooperation. In all, triangulating our dialogue had three (surprise!) advantages. First, this approach was efficient: It enabled us to cut right to the core of many thorny issues. Second, triangulation was cohering: It revealed common strands and structures across seemingly unrelated realms—so we could see how a lot of things fit together. Finally, this method was wonderfully open-ended: The process of triangulating continuously suggested new subjects and concerns worthy of attention.

THE ORGANIZATIONAL DESIGN PROFILE

Chapter 3 has illustrated some ways in which the triangular framework has contributed to organizational planning and design—and thinking. As a result of the experiences presented and a score of other consulting engagements, I have developed an idealized diagnostic framework, the Organizational Design Profile (exhibit 3-9).[9] Typically, the profile has been used to contrast the current state of affairs with a more desirable arrangement. The resulting gap (There *always* is one!) becomes the focus for change, usually initially in terms of one or two of the nine dimensions.

Some caveats. First, there is nothing special about the nine *dimensions* listed in exhibit 3-9. There are scads of similar organizational "checklists," and one's choice of a particular framework makes little difference. What *is* distinctive about the profile, however, is the fact that each dimension is described in terms of autonomy/control/cooperation. Triangular design has been used to integrate McKinsey's 7-S™ *atom*, and it can be similarly applied to unify any other such scheme.[10]

Second, the various dimensions of the Organizational Design Profile overlap, so there is a messiness that cannot be avoided. (The flip side, of course, is positive redundancy: The same organizational aspects may be addressed by several dimensions; hence, the likelihood

Exhibit 3-9

ORGANIZATIONAL DESIGN PROFILE

	AUTONOMY	CONTROL	COOPERATION
STRATEGY			
• **Constituencies** (For whose benefit does this organization exist?)	Customers/ clients	Shareholders/ subsidizers	Employees
• **Character** (What is our essential nature?)	Player-oriented	Coach-oriented	Team-oriented
• **Capabilities** (How do we compete?)	Differentiation (*special*)	Cost (*affordable*)	Flexibility (*adaptable*)
STRUCTURE			
• **Organization Chart** (What is the form of our reporting relations?)	Flat/clear	Steep/clear	Flat/amorphous
• **Layout** (What interaction does our physical design encourage?)	Independent action	Programmed interaction	Spontaneous interaction
• **Interdependence** (How does our work/ information flow?)	Pooled	Sequential	Reciprocal
SYSTEMS			
• **Reward System** (What behaviors are reinforced financially and nonfinancially?)	Individualistic	Hierarchic	Mutual
• **Meeting System** (For what reasons do people get together?)	Forum	Decision-making	Team-building
• **Decision System** (How do we exercise authority?)	Decentralized (*delegate*)	Centralized (*mandate*)	Shared (*collaborate*)

of missing an important concern is lessened.) Third, it is virtually impossible to achieve a perfect fit across all nine dimensions; some will always be "off." Inconsistencies often occur with respect to *capabilities*. As Jeffrey Pfeffer has observed, "Although it may be true that certain types of strategies virtually necessitate the use of high-commitment [autonomy/cooperation] work practices, there is little evidence that such work practices don't also help firms following other strategies such as cost minimization [control]."[11]

Divergence from pattern is as commonplace in organizations as in buildings. According to architect and architectural critic Jonathan Hale, "Harmony in a building means relationships that work with other relationships. A design can have a great deal of discord. In fact, if it doesn't, if there are no mistakes or mutations, the result will be dull."[12] Local conditions or customs may play a major role in producing deviation. Indeed, I consider one or two significant anomalies to be normal—for example, a steep organization chart (control) and/or widely dispersed layout (autonomy) coexisting within a generally cooperative organization.[13]

Because change is relentless, the Organizational Design Profile may best be viewed as a condensed vocabulary for patterning often-novel triangular responses to real-world problems. Chapters 4 through 6 are realistically approached as a framework for *thinking about* organizational dimensions. In particular, one might consider the downside of a one-variable or two-variable perspective on any given dimension (as well as the danger of fixating on a single dimension). For example, are the needs of the organization's three major constituencies—customers *and* shareholders *and* employees—consciously addressed in terms of each other? Are different patterns of interdependence (work/information flow) examined in accordance with varying task requirements? Does the organizational reward system explicitly encourage individualistic *and* hierarchic *and* mutual behaviors, as appropriate? If the answers to such questions are "no," then serious rethinking is in order.

PART 2

Framing Organizational Issues

Organizational Strategy

*"A company's strategic
orthodoxies are
more dangerous than its
well-financed rivals."*

—Gary Hamel and C.K. Prahalad,
"Strategic Intent,"
Harvard Business Review,
May-June 1989

Organizational *strategy* answers three fundamental questions: (1) *why* an organization exists, (2) *what* it is, and (3) *how* it competes. These respective issues are prior to those of organizational *structure* and *systems*. In other words, structure and systems are properly regarded as means for realizing organizational strategy. Nevertheless, an organization may address issues of strategy, structure, and systems in any order—depending on its unique needs, opportunities, and inclinations.

The choices are sketched in exhibit 4-1.

Exhibit 4-1
ORGANIZATIONAL STRATEGY

	AUTONOMY	CONTROL	COOPERATION
• **Constituencies** (For whose benefit does this organization exist?)	Customers/ clients	Shareholders/ subsidizers	Employees
• **Character** (What is our essential nature?)	Player-oriented	Coach-oriented	Team-oriented
• **Capabilities** (How do we compete?)	Differentiation (*special*)	Cost (*affordable*)	Flexibility (*adaptable*)

CONSTITUENCIES

Every organization has three basic constituencies: customers or clients, shareholders or subsidizers, and employees. (And, of course, all three interests reside within an environmental, competitive, and community context.) **Customers** (consumers) exercise the most autonomy because— at least in a free marketplace—they can either take a company's products/services or leave them. **Shareholders** have a control charter: Boards of directors that represent them are legally empowered and expected to control or "direct" their organizations. **Employees,** to be effective, must cooperate—with each other, with management, and with the aims of the enterprise as a whole. What category are managers in? They may fall under shareholders or employees—or both. In fact, the recent push toward splitting the roles of chairman of the board and chief executive officer (CEO) can be interpreted as an attempt to reduce ambiguity about who is in which camp.

How are the three constituencies related? In one sense, customers, shareholders, and employees represent competing forces, and inevitable tradeoffs must be struck. How else can one explain the fact that in

December 1993, immediately after Xerox Corporation announced that it would reduce its workforce by 10,000, its stock shot up 7 percent? Or that in January 1994, right after Scott Paper Co. announced plans to cut its workforce by 25 percent, its stock price jumped 4.9 percent, to a 52-week high (and, indeed, soared in subsequent months as a new CEO announced even more severe personnel cutbacks)?

A 1993 *New York Times* analysis found that many companies appearing on "Most Admired" or "Best Companies to Work for" lists are not exactly great deals for investors: "The companies that receive the highest accolades for management acumen and sensitivity to employees are probably dandy places to work. A rule of thumb for the middle-aged investor, though, might work along these lines: if kindness to employees and lush benefits make it the perfect first job for your college-grad kid, think twice before investing in the stock."[1]

If certain organizations (such as wanton restructurers and downsizers) are one-variable thinkers with respect to shareholders, and others are with respect to employees, then what about customers? Michael Schrage believes that too many companies have deified "customer service" to the extent that they give away the store—often to the *wrong* customer: "Contrary to popular belief, customer service doesn't begin with the customer's expectations of the business—it begins with the business's vision of the customer. Smart businesses pick customers—and learn from them. While some customers consistently add value along several dimensions, other customers are value-subtractors."[2] Schrage's remarks suggest a potentially constructive set of relations among constituencies—an important alternative perspective to that of strict tradeoffs, as identified above.

Ideally—and over the long term, practically—the various constituencies form a kind of *performance cycle* in which committed employees produce satisfied customers, who in turn enrich shareholders (who reinvest in the organization). Clearly, over time there is no way that shareholders will benefit from a company incapable of delivering what its customers want. It is equally apparent that customers will be satisfied only to the extent that the employees who build the products and provide the services are themselves satisfied. As Charles Hampden-Turner has observed, "How products are made and designed must, in the end, depend on how the social systems creating those products are made and designed. Lonely, ugly, and adversarial relationships will result in badly fitting assemblies of junk that shake apart when used—not a bad description of certain British and American automobiles in the recent period of their decline."[3] Exhibit 4-2 diagrams this more optimistic path.

Exhibit 4-2

CONSTITUENCIES PERFORMANCE CYCLE

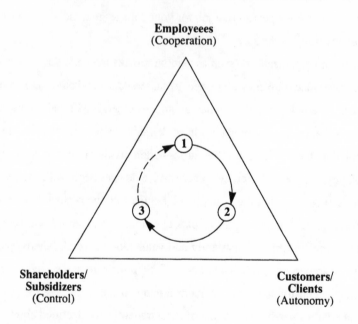

Employeees
(Cooperation)

Shareholders/
Subsidizers
(Control)

Customers/
Clients
(Autonomy)

CHARACTER

Organizational character is identity. What is unique about the organization—and separates it from all other organizations? Character is defined in part by cultural bias—that is, by the overriding social values of the organization. It is also defined by mutual expectations:

what the organization expects from its people, and what people in turn expect from their organization. Finally, character is expressed in terms of an organization's developmental pattern—the manner in which it grows, develops, and renews itself.[4] A summary is given in exhibit 4-3.

Exhibit 4-3

ORGANIZATIONAL CHARACTER

	PLAYER-ORIENTED (Autonomy)	COACH-ORIENTED (Control)	TEAM-ORIENTED (Cooperation)
CULTURAL BIAS	Diversity	Uniformity	Complementarity
ORGANIZATIONAL EXPECTATION	Self-reliance	Compliance	Collaboration
INDIVIDUAL EXPECTATION	Opportunity	Security	Community
DEVELOPMENTAL PATTERN	From the outside	From within	In concert with others

Cultural Bias. Organizations that are biased toward autonomy prize diversity. Such an emphasis is nowhere more apparent than at first-rate colleges and universities. What makes a place top-notch? Smart, well-informed professors and students *who see things differently*. In fact, the quickest way to render a university second-rate is to dampen the range of perspectives it permits.

Historically, top managers like Ed Carlson at United Airlines and John G. McCoy at Banc One went to great lengths to suffuse diversity throughout their corporate cultures. When McCoy took over Banc One in 1959, he resolved to convert what he regarded as a high-quantity "Woolworth" bank into a high-quality "Tiffany" bank. His methods? "Hire people who are exceptional at something and give them some

53

rope." McCoy said that he "would hire the world's best plumber for some position or other if he stumbled across him . . . [and] that if he owned a baseball team, he would have hired Ted Williams 'but I wouldn't tell him how to hold his bat.'"[5]

The opposite pattern is uniformity—comprehending reality in the same way and presenting the same face to the world, irrespective of line of business or geographical location. Corporate identity consultant Wally Olins describes such a presentation pattern as "monolithic identity" and observes that it has been typified by IBM, BMW, Shell, and Yamaha.[6] The danger of monolithic thinking and organizational behavior was recently dramatized by IBM, which clung to its bread-and-butter product, mainframe computers, by continuing to organize in a monolithic, mainframe way.

In fact, in recent years an increasing number of American corporations (including IBM) have for the first time ever appointed outsiders as chief executives—precisely to shake up an entrenched culture of uniformity. At the same time, other organizations as disparate as United Parcel Service and Andersen Consulting continue to find value in uniformity.

Complementarity represents a third perspective on identity. The classic American exemplar is 3M Corporation, whose prevailing belief is that almost any idea will be useful somewhere in the company; hence, few ideas are killed prematurely. Solutions in search of problems may literally wend their way through a gauntlet of different divisions before a match is made. 3M is a firm whose culture appears to match its core technology—bonding.

In the past decade, complementarity has also been expressed outside the organization in terms of what Paul Hawken has called "the ecology of commerce"—environmentally sensitive corporate practices that recognize the many interdependencies between business and other aspects of our world. Thus, Herman Miller, the Knoll Group, and Wal-Mart are willing to pay a premium for timber that is produced in a sustainable manner.[7]

Organizational Expectation. An autonomy-based organization wants people to stand on their own two feet, stick their necks out, and take risks. *The New York Times* editorial page editor Howell Raines describes just such a context: "This is the most demanding professional environment I've ever encountered. . . . The informing idea is 'You're here because you're the best in the business, and the game is on the field. Get on with it.' Our meetings are meant to rip away the details. . . . This is a talent meritocracy. We're not building cars here."[8]

A compliance-based organization expects one to sign up, salute, and march in step. Such companies tend to be secretive and may prevent any employee from talking about the firm publicly. Apropos of this type, Michelin—a supplier to car builders—was characterized in 1990 by *The Wall Street Journal* as follows: "The company's heart, mind and management reside in Clermont-Ferrand, the capital of France's Auvergne region, a place where tightfistedness and suspicion of outsiders are considered virtues."[9]

A commitment to collaboration means neither going off on one's own nor dutifully taking orders. Rather, collaboration means continuously looking for opportunities to assist others—in different jobs, functions, divisions, or locations. Minimills such as Nucor and Chaparral Steel are famous for their workers' ability and willingness to help each other whenever needed.

Individual Expectation. This is the flip side of organizational expectation. Opportunity is the *quid pro quo* for self-reliance in many sales organizations and especially on Wall Street, where earnings are largely a function of commissions. Opportunity may be defined in whatever terms are relevant—financial, promotional, discretionary, and otherwise.

The near-opposite of opportunity is security—the expected payoff for compliant behavior. There are now hundreds of thousands of former middle managers—many with MBA degrees—who are out of work because their companies violated an implicit psychological contract "signed" in the 1950s and 1960s: "Come to work for us, keep your nose clean, and you will be set for life." What happened? The world changed in unforeseen ways. The bargain could no longer be kept.

A third expectation is a strong sense of community—in return for collaborating. The notion is that if one spends half his or her waking life at work, then the workplace should be no less of a caring environment than the home. At the same time, a true concern for community implies that the organization will be sensitive to individual and family needs outside of work.

Developmental Pattern. There are essentially three ways in which an organization can grow or develop: from the outside, from within, or in concert with others. Autonomy-oriented companies tend to favor developing from the outside. MCI, for instance, has long had a practice of filling a significant percentage of job openings at every level with outsiders. That company also welcomes back individuals who had left for a while.

In contrast, control-biased firms believe in doing it all internally, by themselves. A striking historical example is Kodak—at least through the 1980s. In earlier times, Kodak's main Rochester plant even had its own fire department and power plant in order to avoid dependence on the city. Although Kodak and many other old-line firms (such as Alcoa, IBM, and Westinghouse) are avidly trying to change past practices of attempted self-sufficiency, there remain companies committed strictly to internal development. Publix Super Markets, for example, the largest retail food chain in Florida, insists that all employees start at the bottom—as grocery baggers.

Developing in concert with others is a cooperative pattern that has burgeoned in the past decade. The popularity of "benchmarking"—calibrating one's processes and performance against the world's best—is one expression of this dynamic. But most telling is the explosion of joint ventures across every conceivable industry. The progenitor of all corporate alliances is Corning, Inc., which derives about half its earnings from partnerships and describes itself as a "network of organizations."[10] In search of lifetime affiliations, Corning has hooked up with Germany's Siemens, Japan's Mitsubishi, and Mexico's Vitro—not to mention Dow Chemical (in the form of Dow Corning) in the United States, a collaboration that began in 1941.

CAPABILITIES

Organizational performance is a function of three variables: *differentiation* (how distinctive a product/service is); *cost* (how affordable it is); and *flexibility* (how adaptable it is).[11] In general, differentiation derives from organizational/unit/individual autonomy, cost is a function of hierarchical control, and flexibility turns on spontaneous cooperation.[12]

Differentiation is the quality of being special—the extent to which a product/service distinctively meets or exceeds the expectations of the most knowledgeable and selective customers/clients/users—typically in terms of style, performance, and/or novelty. Each of these criteria may encompass several dimensions. For instance, performance in an automobile may refer to speed, handling, durability, and/or safety. Novelty may have to do with the product itself, the way it is packaged, and/or the uses to which it can be put. And style reflects elegance or aesthetics. For example, a Blancpain advertisement proudly proclaims that "Since 1735 there has never been a quartz Blancpain watch. And there never will be."

Cost is the amount that one pays for a product or service. Cost ordinarily has three components:[13] (1) purchase price—that is, the market value of the product/service itself; (2) operating/maintenance cost; and (3) transaction cost—the price for obtaining or disposing of the product/service.

Flexibility usually encompasses (1) responsiveness to customer/client/consumer initiatives; (2) "throughput" speed—loosely, the amount of time it takes for product development or production/service; and (3) malleability—the capacity to change as problems/opportunities emerge.

The differentiation/cost/flexibility triad is depicted in exhibit 4-4.

Exhibit 4-4
CAPABILITY TRIADS

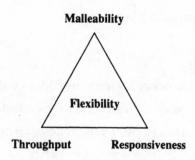

Malleability

Flexibility

Throughput   Responsiveness

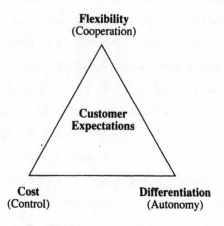

Flexibility
(Cooperation)

Customer
Expectations

Cost   Differentiation
(Control)   (Autonomy)

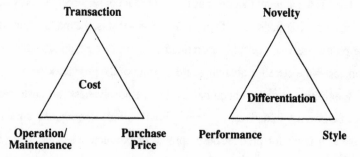

Transaction   Novelty

Cost   Differentiation

Operation/   Purchase   Performance   Style
Maintenance   Price

Differentiation-oriented organizations take pride that no two of their products—whether John Lobb shoes, Chubb insurance policies, or Robert Trent Jones golf courses—are identical. Moreover, the most highly differentiated products and services are almost always the output of individuals—a fact that favors organizational designs based on autonomy. This is equally true in low-tech art and high-tech science. Graphic designer Paul Rand argues that "Design is a personal activity and springs from the creative impulse of an individual. Group design or design by committee, although occasionally useful, deprives the designer of the distinct pleasure of personal accomplishment and self-realization. It may even hinder his or her thought processes, because work is not practiced under natural, tension-free conditions. Ideas have neither time to develop nor even the opportunity to occur."[14] Joel Birnbaum, Hewlett-Packard's vice president of research and development, claims that "In the end, a great idea never comes from some amorphous group. . . . It comes from a person."[15] In the opinion of Cal Tech president Thomas E. Everhart, "One outstanding scientist can do 100 or 1,000 times more good than someone who is almost as good."[16]

Cost-driven organizations—whether jewelry distributor Jan Bell Marketing Inc., office supplier Staples, or steelmaker Allegheny Ludlum—strive for generic processes and outputs that never vary. The design model here is classic control: to render the organization as machinelike as possible by scripting a comprehensive game plan at the top. Cost-reduction techniques are used exhaustively: Put more R&D dollars into process improvements than into product enhancements; use modular product components wherever possible; minimize the material content of products; minimize the number of parts; use inexpensive materials; produce/deliver in high volumes.

Flexibility-oriented organizations are able to combine resources in novel ways. Some of these organizations—like minimarket 7-Eleven and minimill Nucor—excel in terms of speed. The design concept underlying a flexibility strategy is spontaneous cooperation. In a sense, team equals *time*. There is simply no faster way to produce or deliver under changing conditions than through a plastic organization based on multifunctional, self-directed teams. Such a structure minimizes unit/departmental "hand-offs" and hierarchical "checkpoints" by permitting direct communication among relevant specialists and by exercising decision-making authority itself, in real time.

Why do organizational members often seem to pull in diverse direc-tions, instead of coming together in common cause? One reason may be that there are no fewer than twenty-five ways to prioritize differentiation, cost, and flexibility—as set out in exhibit 4-5.[17] Nine responses imply that only two variables are relevant. (For example, CF means that cost and flexibility share the #1 priority; $\frac{C}{F}$ means that cost is #1, and flexibility is #2. In neither case does differentiation matter.) Three responses—D, C, and F—imply one-variable thinking—that only one criterion matters.

Exhibit 4-5

25 WAYS TO PRIORITIZE CAPABILITIES

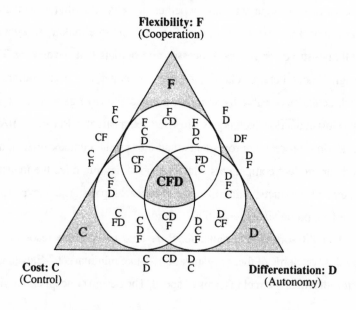

Overdoing differentiation is similar to what management theorist Danny Miller has labeled *tinkering*, a trap to which "Craftsman" organizations are particularly susceptible: "As quality-leader Craftsmen change into Tinkerers, quality, which had been a means of satisfying customers, becomes an end in itself. Quality alone is credited with past success; everything else is ignored. So Tinkerers start to devise indestructible products or pristine services that no one really wants."[18]

Overemphasizing costs has been a common affliction of the early 1990s—with no end of lean-and-mean (anorexic-and-dyspeptic?) strategies. Russell Ackoff got to the heart of the matter when he observed that if a company really wants to minimize costs, it should go out of business: Then it will have no costs.

A highly publicized example of overdoing flexibility—in terms of throughput speed—was Domino's Pizza, which in late 1993 withdrew its 30-minute delivery promise, after a jury awarded $78 million to a woman who had been struck by a Domino's driver. Although Domino's president Thomas Monaghan reiterated his conviction that his firm was "the safest delivery company in the world"[19]—and claimed that he was responding to public perception, not fact—many observers had long regarded Domino's as a one-variable thinker with respect to speed.

Contrast such fixation with Sears, Roebuck & Co. in the late 1980s and early 1990s. Sears appeared bent on representing all things to all people, all the time.[20] It attempted to combine lifetime guarantees on Craftsman tools (differentiation), "everyday low prices" (cost), and a kind of one-stop shopping experience (flexibility) that linked its retail-products business with an array of financial services (stockbroker Dean Witter, real estate broker Coldwell Banker, and insurer Allstate).

Unrealistic expectations abound these days, as it is popular to deny the necessity of striking tradeoffs among performance criteria. No need to compromise quality or efficiency or delivery, we are told. In fact, world-class corporations—like championship sports teams—do perform well across several dimensions, which is another way of saying that they rarely have any glaring weaknesses. But it is naive to suppose that an organization can at once be first-rate in differentiation *and* cost *and* flexibility. The appropriate frame may be a truncated tetrahedron in which performance represents verticality, as depicted in exhibit 4-6 (viewed from above). Accordingly, as competition intensifies (the equivalent in sports of "competing on a higher level," as during post-season playoffs), the tradeoff space becomes smaller. But the triangle still exists and demands prioritization, albeit within tighter parameters.

Exhibit 4-6
DESCRIBING WORLD-CLASS PERFORMANCE:
TRUNCATED TETRAHEDRON

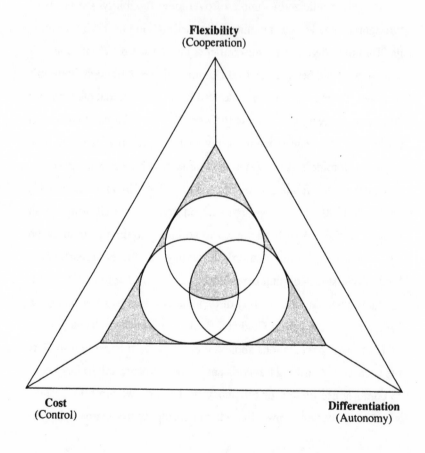

Flexibility
(Cooperation)

Cost
(Control)

Differentiation
(Autonomy)

Some of the most powerful corporate examples of "competing on a higher level"—combining high differentiation, high flexibility (responsiveness to what customers want), and *relative* affordability—are Japanese luxury automobiles such as Honda's Acura Legend, Nissan's Infiniti, and Toyota's Lexus. But $40,000–50,000 per car is hardly "low-cost" (except, perhaps, in comparison with the likes of a high-end Mercedes-Benz).

A concluding note. *Organizational strategy* defines purpose, vision, mission, *raison d'être*. Although the framework presented here is idealized—and therefore vastly oversimplified—it does enable serious dialogue about choices. Too often, corporate purpose is dismissed as something like "the vision thing." But unless an organization periodically thinks through issues of constituencies, character, and capabilities—why we exist, what we are, and how we satisfy customers—the odds are strong that it will lose direction and founder, no matter how rigorously it addresses matters of structure and systems. All of which is to say that organizational strategy has enormous leverage—for better or for worse.

Organizational Structure

"Whole persons aren't contained
in the boxes on organizational charts.
But managers forget that, which is why organizational charts
are never the way things work—
even though people invest enormous time in drawing,
reviewing, pondering, and worrying over them."

—KARL E. WEICK,

The Social Psychology of Organizing, Second Edition

Organizational structure is the hard wiring of design. It—or, more often, *part* of it—is what one-variable thinkers typically have in mind when they conceive of organizational design. Indeed, "structure" for most corporate managers is typically that which is both concrete and clearly visible—the boxes and lines (and levels) that form the organization chart, the physical layout and location of various people and organizational units, and/or the actual work flow.

Exhibit 5-1 summarizes structural dimensions.

Exhibit 5-1
ORGANIZATIONAL STRUCTURE

	AUTONOMY	CONTROL	COOPERATION
• **Organization Chart** (What is the form of our reporting relations?)	Flat/clear	Steep/clear	Flat/amorphous
• **Layout** (What interaction does our physical design encourage?)	Independent action	Programmed interaction	Spontaneous interaction
• **Interdependence** (How does our work/ information flow?)	Pooled	Sequential	Reciprocal

ORGANIZATION CHARTS

A prominent business research group trumpets its organization chart collection of "over 400 leading corporations in 15 major industries [as a way to] keep ahead of your competition."[1] Such a claim may be overstated, but organization charts—pictures of hierarchical reporting relations—can make a difference. The generic alternatives are sketched in exhibit 5-2.

An **autonomy**-oriented chart is flat. To begin with, it contains relatively few levels, or tiers, between the top (CEO/president/executive director) and the bottom (operators/workers/employees). Moreover, it features a substantial "span of control"—that is, the number of people reporting to a given individual. Finally, an autonomy-oriented chart is clear: Individual/unit roles are easy to identify.

A large-scale example is Zurich-based Asea Brown Boveri (ABB), which achieved 1992 revenues in excess of $30 billion with an organization chart of essentially five levels that featured some 5,000 profit centers.[2] Familiar small-scale examples are sales organizations and distributorships made up of only two levels: several individual "offices" that report to a common boss.

Exhibit 5-2

CONTRASTING ORGANIZATION CHARTS

Flat/Amorphous

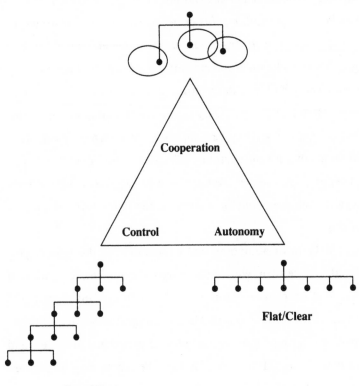

A **control**-oriented chart is also clear, but it is steep: Multiple tiers or steps or ceilings separate the bottom from the top—sometimes as many as nine (or more). And spans of control tend to be minimal. Historically, such charts have been described as *pyramids* or *corporate ladders*. Often they have amounted to vertical mirrors of a long-linked work flow that embodies sequential task interdependence (as will be discussed below).

A **cooperation**-oriented chart is flat but amorphous: Individual/unit reporting relationships tend to be ambiguous and unclear. Indeed, an organization chart as such may not even exist, because the dense interactions among individuals making up the organization defy description—at least in a boxes-and-lines format. Vivid metaphors— such as *lattice organization*, *cluster organization*, *circular organization*, and *spider's web organization*—may better convey such a design. (These and similar patterns are the subject of chapter 8.)

Recall Tracy Kidder's description (cited in chapter 1) of a computer-development group: "Only the simplest visible arrangements existed among them. They kept no charts and graphs or organizational tables that meant anything."[3] Various team-based designs fit this category.[4] In a sense, the team as a whole reports up the hierarchy, although there may be a point person in the form of a leader or liaison.

An amalgam of autonomy and cooperation is the typical professional service firm, which may have only three major groups of professional employees—for example, partners, managers, and associates. Consultant David Maister suggests that in a consulting firm, the groups may be called vice-president, manager, and junior consultant; while in a CPA firm the labels may be partner, manager, and staff. Maister notes that although law firms tend to have only two levels—partner and associate—they typically distinguish (either informally or formally) between senior and junior partners.[5]

Apart from professional service firms, one way to make the contrast between autonomy/cooperation-like charts and those that are control-like is to determine the proportion of managers to workers. The higher the ratio, the more control-like the chart. Political scientist Richard Rosecrance made this kind of analysis in 1990 and discovered that at General Motors, for example, 77.5 percent of the workforce was white-collared/salaried, while only 22.5 percent wore blue collars. Rosecrance also noted that the number of senior military officers was far greater in 1990 than it was at the height of World War II—even though during that war there were six times as many combat troops.[6]

LAYOUTS

An organization's layout is its physical configuration—the ways in which people, machines, buildings, transportation lanes, and other facilities are arranged. Alternative layouts—viable and vulnerable—are graphed in exhibit 5-3.[7]

Exhibit 5-3
LAYOUT PATTERNS

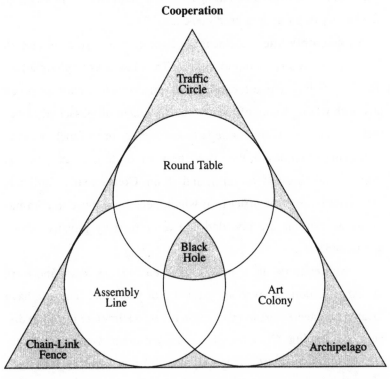

An **art colony** is an arrangement that encourages independent action on the part of employees, as is the case with Silicon Graphics' star engineers, the only members of that company who have enclosed, individual offices.[8] An increasingly popular example of an art colony is a firm made up of computer commuters, each working in his or her house and communicating with the head office via phone, fax, and/or modem. Another example is the family business in which feuding siblings are given geographically separate pieces to manage in order to reduce (if not eliminate) their interactions.

Highly reflective work often calls for an art-colony approach. Yale professor and author Edward Tufte builds independence into his life in order to create: "I can't say that I've learned a lot from my students. I've learned some things, but I've learned a lot more alone in a library or alone in a used book store."[9]

An **assembly line** is a linear configuration that rules in certain interactions, and rules out all others. The classic example is a factory in which machine locations and noise levels dictate who can talk with whom. Many office layouts are essentially assembly lines that call for one position or department to carry out a function (such as logging in requests), then pass the work on to the next position (initial screening and routing), and so on. Conceptually similar is the executive row of offices, in which pecking order and communications patterns are revealed and reinforced by physical space and boundaries.

A **round table** is a setting that encourages back-and-forth exchanges among all who are present. For years, the Japanese have located engineers next to production areas to stimulate informal discussions. Boeing, Chrysler, Steelcase, and other American companies have likewise redesigned layouts in order to bring R&D and operations closer.

In planning its training facility in Virginia, Xerox took explicit steps to ensure that people would interact spontaneously. The building contains zigzagged hallways that literally force people to bump into each other in the course of their internal journeys. And the bedrooms for those in training have no televisions; anyone who wants to watch the tube must do so in a commons area—again, in order to encourage mingling.

An **archipelago** is an art colony overwrought. Not only is independent action encouraged; any kind of interaction is virtually precluded. Tall buildings are especially problematic because of the way they segment the people inside them. Berkeley architect Christopher Alexander and his colleagues have estimated that in terms of human interaction, one story in a building is equivalent to approximately 100 horizontal feet; and that two stories are equivalent to about 300 horizontal feet. Their conclusion: Separate people by two or more floors, and they will have almost no informal contact[10]—therefore, no chances of teaming up.

A **chain-link fence** is an assembly line-type layout that comes to resemble a ratchet—a gear-like wheel with teeth that are canted in one direction so that no backward movement is possible. The most blatant examples of chain-link fences are assembly lines that are run so fast that workers cannot detect a problem when one passes them—even if management has given them the authority to stop the line.

The management equivalent is a physical pattern that severely discourages reciprocal interaction among different disciplines—as, for example, in new-product development. Consequently, R&D designs a product, then lobs its conception over the wall to manufacturing, which is expected to make the product and then lob it over yet another wall to sales/marketing—which is expected to sell it.

A **traffic circle** is a space in which so many people interact so often that almost everyone becomes overwhelmed. The effect is similar to that in an actual traffic circle (rotary), where there is no legal right of way: Cars and trucks continuously cut each other off as they enter and exit. Virtually any organizational unit can degenerate into a traffic circle—if it attracts enough commerce from enough directions. This pattern is particularly evident in departments (or locations) that are lodged between two or more other departments that need to work together closely; the in-between zone becomes inundated from both (all) ends.

A **black hole** is a place where people—and things—disappear. They just seem to get lost. The business school building of a major university with which I am familiar is a good example. The internal arrangement of aisles, offices, and meeting rooms in this structure is so convoluted that both faculty and students find themselves in a constant state of confusion—even after years of navigating the space. One professor aptly described this layout as "a rat psychologist's dream."

INTERDEPENDENCE

Organization charts depict *vertical* reporting relations. Interdependence characterizes work/information flow, or *horizontal* task relations among individuals/organizational units. Much of the current interest in process management, process innovation, and reengineering amounts to making sense of interdependence—from the perspective of customer needs.

As noted earlier (chapter 1, endnote 3), James Thompson articulated the concept of task interdependence by distinguishing three "pure" patterns: pooled, sequential, and reciprocal. Additionally, one can identify three two-way hybrids: spiral, pivotal, and closed-loop. The six patterns are shown graphically in exhibit 5-4.

Exhibit 5-4
INTERDEPENDENCE

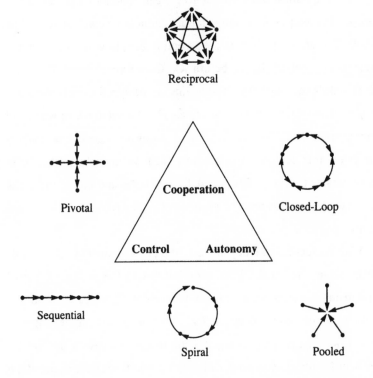

With **pooled** interdependence, organizational parts are relatively independent of each other; each part provides a discrete contribution to the whole system. Individuals/units essentially behave autonomously. In a typical university, for example, at least three levels of pooled interdependence are visible: (1) the particular school or college (business, law, medicine, and so on), (2) various disciplines within each school (marketing, finance, management, and so on), and (3) individual professors within each discipline—many of whom likely have their own satellite research centers.

Conglomerates also exemplify pooled interdependence. Their various units—even if multibillion-dollar entities—represent different products/markets and have little (if anything) to do with each other. Corporate performance is roughly the sum of the units' performances.

With **sequential** interdependence, organizational parts interact in series; each renders an incremental but cumulative contribution to the whole. The archetype here is the assembly line, in which operation A must occur before B, B before C, C before D, and so forth. McDonald's and other fast-food chains are designed exactly the same way, so that operators have little choice about what to do, or when and how to do it. Building construction also follows a sequential path to the extent that certain activities must occur before others (that is, in non-modular patterns). The foundation must be laid before the walls are erected, the walls must be framed before the roof can be built, and so on.

With **reciprocal** interdependence, the parts interact in a back-and-forth manner and make joint contributions to the system. Creative advertising agencies usually reflect this pattern. Historically, an ad was verbally conceived by a copywriter, who then passed on the language to a lower-status artist charged with fitting images to the words. William Bernbach, co-founder of Doyle Dane Bernbach, changed the game from sequential to reciprocal. He forced copywriter and artist to work together as equals in a dynamic exchange, resulting in a final product that was greater than the sum of the words and lines. The quality of ads generated by this interactive process earned Bernbach a reputation as one of the "fathers" of creative advertising.[11]

A *job shop* is a kind of industrial equivalent to a creative ad agency. Such an organization is one in which, by definition, every order may be unique and, therefore, call for a distinctive blend of resources and operations. Several combinations of reciprocal interdependence may be required to process a given job or inquiry.

Spiral interdependence defines a work flow that originates at one point, gradually goes away from this point, and eventually returns to it—but at a higher level. This pattern is more or less described by the expression, "What goes around comes around." The preparation of a formal report often traces a spiral. An individual originates a document, which is then sent out for critical review. Eventually, the report returns to the writer, who responds to others' comments by revising the initial draft.

Pivotal interdependence features one central individual or unit around whom (or which) others interact. It is exemplified by a classic offensive pattern in basketball, in which the center acts as a pivot by receiving the ball from, and passing it to, the other players as they cut toward the basket. A familiar commercial example is a taxicab scheduling system in which a central dispatcher routes individual taxis based on location and availability—and, to some degree, driver preference. This pattern differs from the airline hub-and-spoke arrangement (popularized by Federal Express and now widely used by major carriers) because individual units (cab drivers) have a measure of discretion vis-a-vis the dispatcher and their routes. Drivers are thus similar to cutting guards on a basketball team, who take considerable initiative in interacting with the center and each other.

Closed-loop interdependence describes a pattern in which adjacent individuals or units interact with each other in a manner that ensures complete information exchange, or "coverage" of a work area. For example, Legal Sea Foods, a Boston-area restaurant chain, is organized so that any waiter or waitress may serve a given customer— depending on who is most available. (Tips are pooled and shared equally.) This arrangement promotes flexibility without compromising service in any part of the restaurant.

LIMITATIONS OF DESIGN-AS-STRUCTURE

For most corporate managers, "organizational design" means that which is physical and readily observable: charts, layout, and/or interdependence—who reports to whom, where everyone resides, and how identifiable inputs are converted into identifiable outputs. In other words, the stuff we can see and touch. But organization so defined constitutes an impoverished view of design because it ignores strategy and systems—purposes and processes. It is the tip of the iceberg. Indeed, trying to change structure without carefully attending to issues of strategy and systems is not only naive, but downright dangerous. Organizational systems are the subject of chapter 6.

Organizational Systems

"Every manager is primarily
concerned with generating and
maintaining a network of conversations for action—
conversations in which requests
and commitments
lead to successful completion of work."

—Terry Winograd and Fernando Flores,
Understanding Computers
and Cognition

Organizational systems constitute the soft wiring of design. They are the less visible aspects that nonetheless play a crucial role in determining organizational behavior and performance. Indeed, given the choice of manipulating either structure or systems, most experienced organizational consultants would probably choose the latter.

Three essential systems—those that have to do with rewards, meetings, and decisions—are sketched in exhibit 6-1.

Exhibit 6-1
ORGANIZATIONAL SYSTEMS

	AUTONOMY	CONTROL	COOPERATION
• **Reward System** (What behaviors are reinforced financially and nonfinancially?)	Individualistic	Hierarchic	Mutual
• **Meeting System** (For what reasons do people get together?)	Forum	Decision-making	Team-building
• **Decision System** (How do we exercise authority?)	Decentralized *(delegate)*	Centralized *(mandate)*	Shared *(collaborate)*

REWARD SYSTEMS

Few psychologists would quarrel with the notion that people act in the direction of their own perceived self-interest; hence, organizational reward systems, which significantly overlap organizational character (as discussed in chapter 4), play a central role in influencing behavior. The triangular framework makes it possible to contrast basic types of reward systems, as depicted in exhibit 6-2.

An **individualistic** system values star performers and has an unbalanced pay profile: Outstanding individuals routinely earn more than their bosses. For example, the leading salesperson often brings home more than his or her manager. Similarly, marquee professors' pay tends to outstrip that of university deans, and even presidents. In 1991, for example, a Cornell University professor of surgery pulled in $1.7 million, while that university's president earned $111,131 (although his benefits exceeded this salary).[1]

Wall Street historically has lavished bonuses on top producers, while simultaneously getting rid of marginal brokers and bankers. The philosophy underlying an individualistic system is that a few "heavy hitters" are crucial, while virtually everyone else—especially those whose

Exhibit 6-2
REWARD SYSTEMS

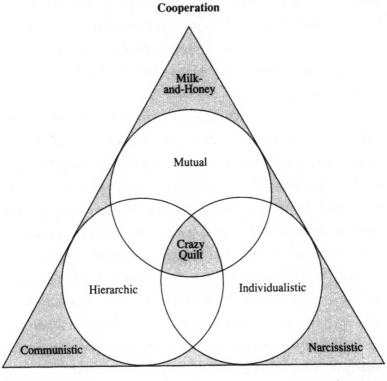

Cooperation

Control   **Autonomy**

performance is average or below-average—is expendable. In many such systems, a large proportion of pay is at risk.

In a **hierarchic** reward system, RHIP—rank hath its *perquisites.* The pay schedule matches the organization chart. Rarely if ever will an individual earn more than her or his boss. The purest examples of such a pattern come from the military and government, where salary levels and corresponding titles form a clean pyramid—from the multitudes at the base, to the chosen few at the apex. Thus the United States government has a twenty-one-rung system: a fifteen-level General Schedule supplemented by a six-level Senior Executive Service. In fact, the fifteen levels of the

General Schedule each contain ten "steps," making for a total of 150 tiers.

A **mutual** reward system features a relatively flat pay profile. In contrast to the federal government, corporate giant GE has only six incentive levels.[2] Steelcase condensed twenty-nine compensation levels into seven groups: four salaried (executive, supervisor/manager, technical/professional, and support/specialist) and three hourly (skilled trade, technical production, and production).

Neither do mutual reward systems have the star-driven extremes of an individualistic (autonomy) pattern. The ratio of top:middle:bottom incomes is sensible and humane. At furniture-maker Herman Miller (#395 among 1994's *Fortune 500*), the CEO's cash compensation cannot exceed twenty times the average factory worker's annual compensation; the chief operating officer's (COO) ratio is limited to 18:1; and other managerial positions are also capped. T.J. Rodgers, founder of Cypress Semiconductor, lives by a policy in which his pay cannot exceed either that of his firm's most highly-paid vice-president, or twenty times that of an entry-level employee.[3] To put these ratios in perspective, in 1993 the average major-company chief executive in the United States was paid approximately 149 times what the average factory worker received.[4]

Mutual reward systems typically encourage *collective* performance. Such arrangements may include gainsharing programs (such as Scanlon or Rucker Plans) or profit-sharing provisions that cover the entire workforce—as at Chrysler. Another form of mutual reward system is the availability of stock options to everybody in the organization—as is now the case at such firms as Du Pont, Merck, PepsiCo, Pfizer, Silicon Graphics, and Tandem Computers.

When the financials go south, a mutual reward system will spread the misery throughout the organization. Nucor Corporation has a "Share the Pain" program in which percentage pay cuts actually increase with hierarchical standing. According to CEO Ken Iverson, "Management should take the biggest drop in pay because they have the most responsibility."[5]

In 1989, Cummins Engine chief executive Henry Schacht not only imposed company-wide pay reductions but docked his own salary 15 percent.[6] And in Japan, when Fujitsu Ltd. struggled in 1992, some executives lost more than one-third of their compensation.[7]

A **narcissistic** system overdoes autonomy to the point that elite players benefit at the expense of their peers, company shareholders, and customers. Wall Street's excesses during the 1980s are the most vivid example of this tendency, as exemplified by Drexel Burnham Lambert, which in 1989 gave individual stars bonuses of more than $10 million each, while the firm lost $40 million.[8]

A **communistic** reward system reserves all of the benefits for those atop the hierarchy. Such a system often relies on "the stick" (punishment) as much as "the carrot"—especially as one goes deep into the organization. Those at the top may win at the same time those at the bottom lose. One of the most publicized instances of this contradictory pattern occurred in 1982 at General Motors. On the same day that the United Auto Workers reluctantly agreed to $2.5 billion in long-term wage concessions, a new top-management bonus scheme was recommended to shareholders.

A **milk-and-honey** reward system exaggerates teamwork and cooperation. Ben and Jerry's Homemade, the ice cream company, has had to *reduce* pay equity in its hierarchy in order to recruit top-notch people. Next Computer faced the same problem, only in a more severe form. When Steve Jobs started that firm in the mid-1980s, he slotted everybody into one of two (annual) pay levels: $75,000 or $50,000. Jobs had to scrap this excessively egalitarian policy in order to attract talented individuals.[9]

Milk-and honey reward systems tend to place all employees' interests clearly ahead of customers' (and shareholders'). At the teaching hospital of an Ivy League university, parking garage attendants are given reserved spaces at or near the entrance to the building. Patients, meanwhile, must often spiral their cars up and down several levels in order to locate a vacant spot—probably on the roof.

A **crazy-quilt** reward system is a muddle. Pay levels are unclear—or ever-changing. The relative importance of individual, unit, and organizational performance to one's paycheck may be unspecified—perhaps because of confusion about what mix of individual initiative, technical contribution, and collegial behavior is desired. Crazy-quilt reward patterns are not uncommon in fast-growing, privately-owned businesses—especially when pay levels are determined in an ad hoc manner by an eccentric entrepreneur/founder. Chaotic reward systems are also found in public corporations that have expanded via multiple mergers/acquisitions but have failed to integrate the disparate compensation schemes.

MEETING SYSTEMS

If one were to gather most managers' honest impressions about meetings, it is likely that some four-letter words would be aired. Meetings, by and large, are the object of derision and scorn. They are the fodder for tongue-in-cheek articles such as Stanley Bing's "Sure Cures for the Madness of Meetings,"[10] and books such as Stephen Baker's *I Hate Meetings*—a collection of verbal and visual cartoons.[11] One individual I know refers to her weekly staff meeting as a "staph infection." Yet as Intel CEO Andrew Grove has argued, "A meeting is nothing less than the *medium* through which managerial work is performed."[12] Moreover, every organization's meetings form a "meeting system"[13] that can be readily analyzed and, if necessary, changed.

Aside from education and training, there are three good reasons for a group of people to meet at work: (1) to create a forum, (2) to make decisions, and (3) to build a team.[14] A **forum** is an opportunity for individuals with different values, concerns, and experiences to share their perspectives and learn from each other. It may range from a loosely assembled "town meeting" to a tightly-structured colloquium. It may also constitute the first stage of a brainstorming process—freewheeling idea-generation. Whatever its details, a forum is characterized by *di*vergence; its product is typically a set of issues, ideas, or agendas.

A **decision-making** meeting is intended to produce direction for the organization or unit. Certain alternatives will be ruled in and others ruled out. The subject of such a meeting may range from strategy or policy formulation to problem solving. Or it may constitute the second stage of brainstorming—hardnosed evaluation. In any case, a decision-making meeting represents a group's exercise of choice—its *con*vergence on one or more objectives and/or courses of action.

A **teambuilding** meeting develops group capabilities—in particular, interpersonal and organizational skills. Such a meeting may also help instill a sense of togetherness and a commitment to collective performance, especially with regard to an agreed-upon path. Meetings that recognize and celebrate team effort and achievement also serve a teambuilding function.

The three types of meetings form the cycle shown in exhibit 6-3.

Exhibit 6-3
MEETING CYCLE

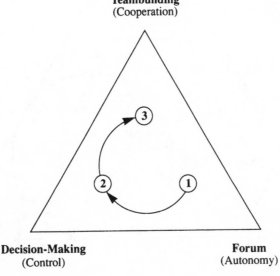

Teambuilding
(Cooperation)

Decision-Making
(Control)

Forum
(Autonomy)

A forum identifies issues and options that provide the grist for a decision-making meeting, at which the group zeroes in on a course of action. Teambuilding then helps the group implement its chosen path.[15]

Unfortunately, too many corporate meetings are **info-dumps**—convened for the sake of information exchange, which is more efficiently handled by phone or fax, or through the mail (physical or electronic). At one retail company, for example, sector managers routinely summoned together their geographically dispersed direct reports—as many as forty—and then proceeded to read memos aloud. In another firm, a similar practice gave rise to a new middle-management metaphor: "the

Exhibit 6-4

MEETING SYSTEMS

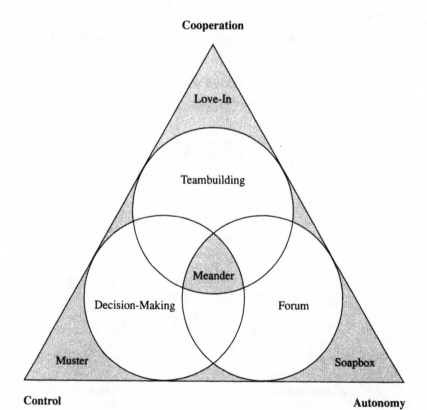

human bulletin board." Still other corporate meetings amount to either a perversion of one of the three legitimate types or an amorphous admixture.

The array of meeting types (excluding info-dumps) can be triangulated (exhibit 6-4). A **soapbox** is a meeting in which one or more individuals sound off or "grandstand." Unlike a forum, a soapbox—whatever its shape and size—is not concerned with learning. On the contrary, it is likely to be an exercise in exhibitionism. The worst examples of this genus that I have ever experienced were, paradoxically, university faculty meetings—where egos ran rampant. Certain professors and administrators would drone on interminably, as though captivated by the sound of their own voice. I used to sit in these sessions and ask myself where I would rather be: at that meeting or sitting in a dentist's chair, having my teeth (instead of my ears) drilled. I was unable to decide which lot was worse.

A **muster** is a roll call in which attendance and obedience are the name of the game. The convener of such an assembly is more interested in displaying his or her power to force others to show up than in accomplishing anything. Deference and passivity are required behaviors. Some musters even turn into floggings—psychological canings that would do Singapore proud. Like all other types of meetings, a muster may occur at any organizational level. Although the metaphor conjures up images of "non-skilled" military grunts rigidly at attention, the executive suite is amply represented. Thus the financial vice-president of a *Fortune* 500 corporation told *The Wall Street Journal* that his former CEO "always did a lot of work ahead of you so that . . . meetings were held not to figure out what to do but to tell you what to do."[16]

A **love-in** is a teambuilding meeting in which concerns about people's feelings are allowed to overwhelm concerns about tasks. The process consumes the product. All that matters is that everybody be nice to everybody else. I'm OK, you're OK, we're OK—hooray! Conflict is avoided at all costs. In such a get-together, tangents are highly valued because they provide an easy way to leave an uncomfortable subject and refocus on something else that is less threatening.

A **meander** is a random walk through various meeting types, both positive and negative. The meeting jumps from one pattern to another, without signal. People attending such a meeting are typically at cross purposes and have disparate (hidden) agendas. There will rarely be any cumulative development through the session. If polled after such a gathering has ended, individuals will differ markedly about why the meeting was held and what it did or did not accomplish.

Soapboxes, musters, and love-ins are usually the products of one-variable thinkers—individually or collectively—who by definition see only a single way of doing things. Meanders, which reveal a total inability to make sense of complexity, reflect undifferentiated thinking.

DECISION SYSTEMS

If many managers' knee-jerk reaction to "meetings" is negative, the typical response to "decision-making" borders on reverential. In fact, the latter topic has spawned no end of formal academic treatises replete with complex equations, decision trees, and payoff matrices. Even though many of these tomes are incomprehensible to the practicing manager, their existence seems to validate decision-making as a subject.

Like rewards and meetings, decisions can be organized into a system—which can then be analyzed and revised as organizational members see fit. Most decision-making options can be expressed in terms of exhibit 6-5.

Exhibit 6-5
DECISION SYSTEMS

Cooperation

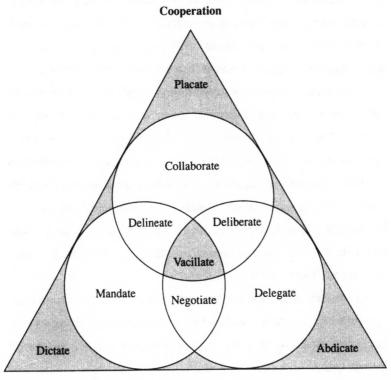

Control   **Autonomy**

"Pure" Modes of Decision-Making

There are six viable ways to make a decision—three "pure" and three mixed—and four nonviable modes. The "pure" patterns and their flawed extremes will be discussed first.

To **delegate** a decision is to permit one or more subordinates to decide within boundaries set by the manager. Delegation is a form of empowerment that has three strengths: (1) It moves authority close to the action—real-time, real-place; (2) it increases subordinates' ownership of the decision; and (3) it frees up the delegator's time for more strategic decision-making.

87

But delegation has a flip side. First, this mode assumes subordinate managerial/technical competence and the desire to exercise authority—all of which may be unwarranted. Second, delegation may ignore connections among subordinates or the organizational units that they head. When in doubt, a manager should verify people's competence, motivation, and understanding of linkages before relinquishing authority.

To **abdicate** a decision is to wash one's hands of responsibility—a pattern that amounts to abandonment rather than empowerment. AT&T's Universal Card Services division made this mistake early in its existence. Senior managers understood that Universal's telephone representatives would need to exercise significant authority in order to meet customer requests on the spot. According to Rob Davis, chief quality officer, "We had thought that by saying, 'You are empowered,' the associates would step up to the plate and take care of everything. . . . What we missed is that we hadn't given them all the tools."[17]

To **mandate** a decision is to make the call unilaterally. When a manager mandates, she or he usually brings to bear a global perspective—the big picture. And mandating is easy to do since no one else is involved in the process.

The downside of a global perspective is an insensitivity to local conditions—the nitty-gritty. And the price of an easy decision-making process is that those left to implement the decision may lack energy. Few people feel ownership of a decision when they have played no part in arriving at that decision.

To **dictate** is to impose orders—what to do/how to do it—without explaining *why*, and without concern for subordinates' reactions. Over the past few years, many corporate "downsizings" have been dictated, and many of these have failed—at least in part because managers have been unable to show why the cuts were strategically important and what roles the surviving employees could expect to play in the new, slimmed-down organization.[18]

The difference between mandating and dictating—and their contrasting effects—verges on the difference between *decisive* and *derisive*. Consider the experience of a firm that, because of financial difficulties, imposed a 10-week, 15 percent pay cut on personnel at two of its facilities.[19] In the first plant, managers announced the action but did not explain why it was necessary. In the second plant, managers discussed the reasons for the reduction, indicated that pain was being shared by everyone, and suggested that the pay cut was an alternative to layoffs. The consequences? In the first plant, thefts by employees nearly tripled; in the second plant, thefts barely rose at all and then fell back to their historical level.

To **collaborate** is to decide jointly with subordinates (and perhaps peers) through a consensual process. Consensus has three components: (1) Each group member has the opportunity to present his/her perspective; (2) the group systematically structures and evaluates multiple options; and (3) everyone commits to implementing the group's preferred course of action. Thus, for example, suppose that a group generates five alternatives—A, B, C, D, and E—and determines that two of these—say, B and D—are the most workable. A particular group member's own first choice is B, but the will of the group is D. That individual goes along with D since he/she has had a say *and* can freely support the chosen path.

Collaboration has two equally important strengths: It brings multiple perspectives and resources to bear on an issue or decision or problem, and it virtually guarantees that the group or team will be committed to implementation. The weaknesses, however, are not insignificant. True collaboration can be a time-consuming and frustrating process—especially for those unfamiliar with this pattern. (Yet, as will be pointed out later, collaboration can paradoxically become a fast decision process when it is intelligently combined with mandate—or delegation.[20]) Collaboration is also difficult with large numbers of people; the ideal group size is about five to eight. Finally, a collaborative style of decision-making requires both interpersonal and technical competence—as well as a willingness to participate.

To **placate** is to pacify—to prevent or dampen discord and emotion. The process of decision-making becomes more important than the decisions at hand. In an effort to keep everyone happy, decisions are either avoided or made subject to unanimous approval.

Mixed Modes of Decision-Making

There are four mixed decision-making patterns. One of these, negotiation, is useful under certain conditions. Another, vacillation, is unworkable. The remaining two modes—delineation and deliberation—are unfamiliar to most managers but represent important patterns for the future.

To **negotiate** is to compromise—to split the difference between two alternatives, or in other words, to strike a balance or "average" between two poles. Negotiation can be an efficient way to resolve differences—as opposed to conflict (for example, in the form of a strike)—because the process is clear-cut and usually perceived as "fair," since each side gives up something ("pain-sharing") to reach an agreement.

Negotiation's downside stems from the linear nature of compromise. This mode tends to produce unimaginative decisions and solutions because it settles for the *average* of A and B $[(A + B)/2]$, instead of either synthesizing A and B (AB) or introducing a third variable (C) into the equation (triangular thinking).

Another difficulty with negotiation is that it usually fails to inspire commitment to implementation. Neither party to a compromise is likely to be excited about the end result. The feeling is similar to that of having played a hard-fought football or soccer game and ending up with a tie.

To **vacillate** is to lurch from one decision-making pattern to another with no rhyme or reason. Managers whose primary style is vacillation either fail to understand decision-making options and their respective advantages/disadvantages and are forever trying to compensate for the problems that their latest style has wrought, or they delight in "test driving" the latest management fad to come their way.

To **delineate** a decision requires three steps: (1) To collaborate in generating an agenda and a set of relevant options, (2) to attempt to reach consensus on a particular option, but (3) if that process fails, to mandate a decision. This pattern is based on the work of Stanford professor Kathleen Eisenhardt, who studied eight microcomputer firms to discover how executives make decisions in fast-changing environments.[21] Eisenhardt found that, paradoxically, fast-deciding organizations used more information and developed more options than slow-deciding organizations; the fast decision-makers also outperformed their slower counterparts.

At the heart of fast decision-making is a two-tiered process that Eisenhardt terms *consensus with qualification*: "First, a team attempts to reach consensus by involving everyone. If agreement occurs, the choice is made. However, if consensus is not forthcoming, the CEO and, often, the relevant VP make the choice, guided by input from the entire team. . . . [As one vice-president put it,] 'Most of the time we reach consensus, but if not, Randy [the CEO] makes the choice.'"

The fast decision-makers' success is explained by a host of factors related to their management of a decision *system*. First, these teams make extensive use of real-time operational information and prefer real-time communication (face-to-face or electronic mail) to slower, more formal means. Such behavior, according to Eisenhardt, "speeds issue identification, allowing executives to spot problems and opportunities sooner."

Second, continuously adapting to current information helps the fast-deciders develop their intuition about the business and its environment. Third, "constant attention to real-time information may allow executive teams to gain experience in responding as a group. The frequent review of real-time information may develop the social routines people need to respond rapidly when pressing situations arise."

Eisenhardt goes on to note that "rapid decisions were characterized by simultaneous consideration of multiple alternatives, and the slower decisions were characterized by sequential consideration of fewer alternatives." In Eisenhardt's study, faster and higher-performing top management teams considered, on average, 3.2 strategic alternatives; slower and lower performers, 2.0. In thinking terms, the faster decision-makers appeared to use *triangular* patterns, while the slower group probably applied two-variable patterns. (Given the technological sophistication of the computer industry, one-variable thinking would likely have been suicidal.)

Eisenhardt's findings about rapid decision-making suggest a parallel with chess playing. Nobel laureate Herbert Simon has proposed the following experiment.[22] Show both a grandmaster and a novice an actual chess game with about twenty-five pieces on the board; then after five to ten seconds, remove the pieces and ask the two to reconstruct what they saw. According to Simon, the grandmaster will replace twenty-three to twenty-four pieces accurately, while the novice will average about six pieces.

Now repeat the challenge, this time with the chess pieces arranged randomly. The results: "The novice can still replace about 6 pieces and the grandmaster—about 6!" Simon explains the experiment's results as follows:

For the expert . . . a chess board is not an arrangement of 25 pieces but an arrangement of a half dozen familiar patterns, recognizable old friends. On the random board there are no such patterns, only the 25 individual pieces in an unfamiliar arrangement.

The grandmaster's memory holds more than a set of patterns. Associated with each pattern in his or her memory is information about the significance of that pattern—what dangers it holds, and what offensive or defensive moves it suggests. Recognizing the pattern brings to the grandmaster's mind at once moves that may be appropriate to the situation. It is this recognition that enables the professional to play *very strong chess at a rapid rate* [emphasis added]. Previous learning that has stored the patterns and the information associated with them in memory makes this performance possible.

By analogy, Eisenhardt's fast decision-makers were business grandmasters who considered a given decision in the context of all other relevant decisions. And since the process was group-based, the management team in each case developed a rich organizational memory; it became a trove of possible responses to potential challenges.

As positive and encouraging a process as delineation may be, it has two related vulnerabilities. First, the top manager's consideration of others' ideas may be perfunctory; that is, the team leader may be tempted to pull the trigger too quickly. Second, should the latter pattern become chronic, other team members will likely become cynical about their *pseudo*participation—a danger that consultation always carries with it. Such disillusionment came to afflict a large technical organization I observed, whose leader proudly informed me that he believed "in the participative method of *ruling* people."

Or consider the U.S. Postal Service's initial response to mounting outbreaks of violent behavior on the part of distressed postal employees. (Between 1986 and 1991, five separate shooting incidents resulted in the deaths of twenty-six people.) In order to provide counseling to troubled workers, the postal service established an 800 telephone number that anyone could presumably call to talk with a therapist. But this number was initially staffed with only a single individual! One can imagine the effect of a repeated busy signal on somebody already at the brink.

To **deliberate** a decision is to "network" it over time so that eventually, the resulting choice reflects the best mix of individual and group thinking. Put another way, deliberation is a pattern of decision-making that represents a symmetrical blend of delegation and collaboration. This pattern is derived from a concept articulated by Calvin Pava, who defined deliberations as "reflective and communicative behaviors concerning a particular topic. They are patterns of exchange and communication in which people engage with themselves or others to reduce the equivocality of a problematic issue."[23]

Deliberating contrasts with delineating in three respects. First, the *players* differ. In a delineating pattern, the players consist of a discrete management team and its leader. In a deliberation, the players are likely to come from diverse parts and levels of the organization (and sometimes outside it) and collectively form a loose network.

Second, the players' *roles* differ. In a delineation, the roles of top manager, senior functional adviser, and team member are clear at the outset. In a deliberation, appropriate roles are not specified up front, but evolve over time. According to Pava, "for any topic, a unit's [an individual's] contribution might range from commentary or consultation to final decision-making."

Third, the *process* differs. Delineations follow a sequential, convergent, group-based pattern that moves from collaboration to mandate (if necessary). By contrast, deliberations feature a nonlinear trajectory that cycles back and forth between divergence and convergence, and balances group and individual contributions.

Much of the difference in process reflects a different treatment of time. Whereas delineations appear to channel time into a specific agenda and decision, deliberations seem to generalize time across several agendas and decisions. The contrast may be summed up as *fast* consulting versus *slow* consulting (as implied by the word *deliberate*)—a potential vulnerability of deliberation.

But over a long time frame, slow may actually be fast—as the

Japanese R&D practice of "parallel development" illustrates. Parallel development is a commitment to building not one new product but three, so that as soon as the competition matches the first generation of the new offering, a second generation can hit the market, and so on. Pulling off this challenge requires all manner of flexibility, boundary crossing, and mutual understanding. Thus at Sony, senior managers and division managers regularly attend R&D meetings. As a result, R&D remains connected to the real world, while operating units stay in touch with emerging technology that may be relevant to their products.[24]

One caveat. To deliberate does not mean to *vote*—another form of decision-making that could fall midway between "delegate" and "collaborate" on the triangle. A voting process is simple and usually perceived as fair ("democratic"). Such a decision mechanism is particularly useful as a way to winnow an abundance of information, especially electronically (in which case, voting can be interpreted as a subset of deliberation). But voting has severe limitations as a primary decision-making pattern in an organization. First, this process assumes that all have equal or equivalent knowledge/expertise. Second, voting permits little or no opportunity for exchanging premises, ideas, and concerns. Third, and most important, voting can very quickly polarize a team into pro and con, majority and minority, winners and losers.[25]

ON STRATEGY AND SPEED

Under severe time constraints, *delineation* appears quite sensible. But the more strategic an issue or a decision, the more critical it is that all relevant perspectives are brought to bear—often including the temporal perspective, that is, the opportunity for alternative points of view to intermingle over time. By *strategic*, I mean a choice that is nonroutine, high-risk, expensive, long-term, relatively irreversible, and organization-wide in its implications. As Ian Mitroff and Harold Linstone have argued, *"Far better to debate a question without necessarily settling it than to settle a question without debating it.* While we understand and empathize with the need for executives to take decisive action, it is better to delay than to take the wrong actions for the sake of expediency."[26]

Deliberation holds special promise because it integrates (1) different points in time, (2) varying degrees of organizational membership (it often incorporates the insights of "key outsiders"), and (3) individual and collective interpretations. These linkages are as essential in research as they are in management. Given the increasing interdependence of scientific disciplines, collaborative inquiry is becoming the norm. Thus, while in 1973 most of the world's scientific and engineering papers were authored by one or two people, by 1986 the majority reflected the collaboration of three or more.[27]

A recent editorial in *Science* argues that "the new reality is that scientists who desire to be on the cutting edge must keep apace of techniques in other disciplines as well as in their own fields. . . . Scientists of the future must parlay their meeting currency in order to buy techniques across the spectrum of science—to expand their problem-solving skills beyond the immediate horizons and participate in the revolution of technology that will most assuredly follow."[28]

In sum, the necessary bias is toward a symmetrical combination of autonomy and cooperation, and away from traditional Western tendencies to control—by mandating and even dictating. This new blend represents a relatively nonhierarchical way to overcome one of the major limitations of a highly cooperative design—size constraints. The autonomy/cooperation hybrid is the subject of chapter 8. Before examining this model at greater length, however, the more fundamental concept of an organizational pattern language is explicated in chapter 7.

PART 3

Designing
for Tomorrow

Toward an Organizational Pattern Language

*"The mind-set of the theoretical scientist is useful
not only for probing the ultimate secrets of the universe but for
many other tasks as well. All around us are facts that are
related to one another. Of course, they can be regarded as
separate entities and learned that way. But what a difference
it makes when we see them as part of a pattern! Many facts then
become more than just items to be memorized—their
relationships permit us to use a compressed description,
a kind of theory, a schema, to apprehend and remember them.
They begin to make some sense. The world becomes a
more comprehensible place."*

—MURRAY GELL-MANN, *THE QUARK AND THE JAGUAR*

Conventional approaches to organizational design and change are, at best, linear. Many are rooted in Kurt Lewin's famous three-step process of unfreeze/move/refreeze.[1] Some change constructs resemble a mathematical *permutation*—in which the order of a set of elements is critical. Managers are advised to work on stage (or phase or track) A first, B second, C third, and so on. The obvious difficulty with such a tack is the assumption that organizational contexts are sufficiently similar that a single trajectory can (and should) be specified for all.

A more robust perspective is to view the change process as a *combination*—in which the order of elements in a set is irrelevant. What matters is that eventually, all elements are addressed (and integrated) in a way that makes sense for a particular organization. Such is the approach I have typically used in diagnosing organizations and proposing alternative courses of action. But even this method has proved to be problematic because of the pace and severity of change impinging on the design effort. Any extended sequence of activities (in whatever order) is likely to be undercut by uncontrollable events long before it reaches completion.[2] Scripting even a three- or four-phase process may therefore be unrealistic. In a variety of projects of which I am aware, before a third stage could be carried out key players resigned/retired/relocated, whole organizational units were eliminated, and/or established markets were abandoned.

Under such conditions, it gradually became evident that what managers really need is a powerful *language*—a way of perceiving, thinking, and communicating—that they can apply to all manner of issues and problems, many of which arrive unannounced, at once. Indeed, the fundamental change issue may have less to do with any apparent gap between actual and desired states than with the way we *conceptualize* these (and interim) states.

To use a metaphor from the martial arts, managers need a kind of *conceptual karate*. Unlike boxers, for example, karate experts fight in 360 degrees and use all of their mind and body as resources. Equally important, they are able to apply complex fighting patterns, known as *kata*, in which they have trained exhaustively. A kata is "a series of defensive and offensive moves against imaginary attacks from differ-ent directions;"[3] some kata contain more than sixty discrete steps. In an actual fight, pieces of various kata are combined flexibly, as need-ed. The Shotokan karate expert thus learns a deep language—physical, verbal, and graphic (and spiritual)—that enables him or her to respond creatively and effectively to virtually any contingency. (I know a little about karate from having observed my son, Andy—a second-degree black belt—train.)

A PATTERN LANGUAGE

Surprisingly similar to karate's system of kata is the concept of a design/construction *pattern language*, as developed by Christopher Alexander, et al.[4] Alexander and his coauthors define 253 patterns that characterize the world's most beautiful, functional, and enduring phys-ical structures: "Each pattern is a three-part rule, which expresses a relation between a certain context, a problem, and a solution. . . . Patterns can exist at all scales."[5] For example, one pattern is *building complex*, about which Alexander et al. say the following:

> A building cannot be a human building unless it is a complex of still smaller buildings or smaller parts which manifest its own internal social facts. . . . Therefore:
>
> Never build large monolithic buildings. Whenever possible translate your building program into a building complex, whose parts manifest the actual social facts of the situation. At low densities, a building complex may take the form of a col-lection of small buildings connected by arcades, paths, bridges, shared gardens, and walls.
>
> At higher densities, a single building can be treated as a build-ing complex, if its important parts can be picked out and made identifiable while still part of one three-dimensional fabric.

Even a small building, a house for example, can be conceived as a "building complex"—perhaps part of it is higher than the rest with wings and an adjoining cottage.[6]

The organizational equivalent of a physical pattern is an issue that can be expressed as a relation among autonomy, control, and cooperation. One may thus regard the contents of the Organizational Design Profile (exhibit 3-9) and appendix B as a rudimentary pattern language. These triads form an elemental vocabulary, any parts of which can—in response to a current issue or concern—(1) be applied "off the shelf," (2) be revised/reformulated as appropriate, or (3) be used to stimulate or uncover entirely new triads.

With respect to the third option—stimulating/uncovering new triads—there is another, more open-ended sense in which one may speak of architectural and organizational patterns. Jonathan Hale, in *The Old Way of Seeing*, has argued that the essence of architecture is patterns of a less specific nature—compelling relationships based on light and shade, proportion, and geometric forms. Hale puts particular emphasis on discerning geometric patterns by superimposing "regulating lines"—straight lines (often diagonals) that connect critical points—on a building's likeness: "To explore the regulating lines in a building is to delve into the guiding thoughts, the connections, the happy coincidences, that make up its design, for these lines organize the geometry of forms. The lines are usually, but not always, hidden. . . . When we analyze a building, the regulating lines show up like the tracks of particles in a cloud chamber, traces of the designer's ordering thoughts."[7]

For Hale, a pattern "language" would appear to be a largely implicit, intuitive body of design insights that help make sense of a building *after* its design has begun (and in many cases, been completed). For Alexander, such a language is an explicit, systematic set of principles to be applied from the very start of design. In organizational terms,

Hale's perspective is biased toward diagnosing what *is*, while Alexander's has to do with creating what *will be*. But the commonalities dwarf the contrasts. And both concepts of patterning differ markedly from most current allusions to *organizational architecture*, which liken organizations to buildings.[8] The organization-as-building trope helps to make organizational design concrete, but it has two serious shortcomings: Buildings are biased for stability, whereas organizations should be biased for change; and architecture, at least as traditionally practiced in the West, tends to be a top-down affair[9] (and indeed, an outside-in process, as few architects ever live in the buildings they design).

Ironically, the precepts of Christopher Alexander and Jonathan Hale—both of whom are practicing architects—are more flexible and participative than those of many management writers who attempt to exploit the architecture analogy.[10] Alexander notes that "Architects are responsible for no more than perhaps 5 percent of all the buildings in the world."[11] One wonders if, similarly, CEOs are responsible for a like proportion of organizational design—which would leave enormous responsibility in the heads and hearts and hands of all others. But more to the point, Alexander's and Hale's work suggests that organizational design can usefully be compared to art as well as to architecture. The essential difference is that architecture constrains people, whereas art does not. Buildings affect all who are either inside them or near (within view of) them. By contrast, art exerts no such force; one can either take it or leave it.[12] Art is thus *variety-increasing*, while architecture tends to be *variety-decreasing*.[13]

Metallurgist Cyril Stanley Smith reinforces Alexander's approach. While he acknowledges the importance of "analytical atomism" in understanding complexity, Smith argues that "the richest aspects of any large and complicated system arise in factors that cannot be measured easily, if at all. For these, the artist's approach, uncertain though it inevitably is, seems to find and convey more meaning."[14]

Moreover, art can be learned and "done" by everyone. It may not be coincidental that Christopher Alexander recently published a book titled *A Foreshadowing of 21st Century Art: The Color and Geometry of Very Early Turkish Carpets*. In it, Alexander stresses the importance of graphic configurations (in the carpets) that he calls *centers*, and emphasizes that a center is defined "by its place *in the whole visual field*, and by the way in which the various elements in the field cooperate to produce a feeling of intensity and centrality at some particular point." Alexander goes on to note that *"every carpet contains hundreds, in many cases even thousands of centers, strewn, packed, and interlocked, throughout its structure. . . .* it is in this concept of a multiplicity of overlapping centers, that the power of the concept lies."[15]

Just as a carpet has myriad centers, so does (or should) every organization. Similarly, just as each carpet is, in Alexander's words, "a picture of God" created in the mind of its weaver, so should each organizational member create and pursue his or her own vision of the organization—in the context of a generally-shared vision. Indeed, articulating an overarching yet open vision may be senior management's essential architectural, or framing, task—within which substantial "organizational art" is possible.[16] Such a notion recognizes that each organizational member has a unique perspective, every perspective has value, and managers' "architectural intelligence" consists in large part of recognizing individual distinctiveness, matching different perspectives with different organizational needs, and blending all perspectives into a coherent but evolving whole.

ON TRIADS

Annemarie Schimmel has acknowledged the importance of *three* in theology and philosophy, and linked the trinity to a human tendency for grouping things in threes: "The widespread idea of a triune deity shows that it must have deep-rooted foundations in the human mind. As early as the Middle Ages, Albertus Magnus . . . claimed that 3 is in all things and signifies the trinity of natural phenomena."[17] Schimmel goes on to quote Lao-tzu: "The Tao produces unity, unity produces duality, duality produces trinity, and the triad produces all things."[18]

Am I suggesting that only through triangular thinking can one make intelligent organizational design decisions? Certainly not. In fact, there are several powerful theoretical approaches detailed in the literature that are based on two-variable thinking. Equally, there are effective "polygonal" methodologies—involving four or more variables. So there are and always will be other workable ways of thinking about organizations.

I do believe, however, that triangular thinking is more *efficient* than these alternatives because it models the nature of organization itself. In this respect, triangular thinking is the cognitive and social equivalent of what Buckminster Fuller discovered about the natural world: "Nature needs only triangles to identify arithmetical 'powering' for the self-multiplication of numbers. Every square consists of triangles. Therefore, 'triangling' is twice as efficient as 'squaring.' This is what nature does because the triangle is the only structure. If we wish to learn how nature always operates in the most economical ways, we must give up 'squaring' and learn to say 'triangling.'"[19]

One caution, however: *Triangular* and *triadic* are not always synonymous. Certain individuals who do think in threes tend to array triads along a mental continuum. But doing so is dangerous because it reduces qualitative difference to quantitative difference. Although he generally advocates preparing *three* different scenarios of the future, Peter Schwartz voices a concern about this number: "There is a common trap with three scenarios: it is easy to offer a bland assortment in which one represents the high road, one the low road, and one the average of the two. . . . I try to make the third path a little bit off-the-wall, to avoid a business-as-usual path."[20]

Or consider the complex concept of interdependence (discussed in chapter 5), which is often expressed in terms of a low/high continuum. Such a translation reduces a fundamental triad (three qualitatively different patterns: pooled, sequential, and reciprocal) into a linear degree-of-interaction scale. In general, this kind of conversion is problematic because it trivializes reality, or possible realities. Instead of considering blends of three options—A, B, and C—one restricts thinking to blends of two—A and B.

Intuitively, triangular thinking makes sense. The acid test of any concept is its comprehensibility to young children. In 1991, I presented triangular design to my daughter's second-grade class. I drew three triangles on the blackboard and labeled them "play," "school," and "family," respectively. We then discussed the meaning of *autonomy* ("doing whatever you want"), *control* ("setting/following rules"), and *cooperation* ("helping each other out"). The kids had no difficulty identifying and explaining the different blends in each realm.

The concept of triangular design has three features that go to the heart of management and organization—and language: incompleteness, integration, and stickiness. Triangular design is forever *incomplete* because there will always be new aspects of organization to pattern—as well as other ways to pattern existing aspects. Twenty-five hundred years ago, Heraclitus observed that "You could not step twice into the same rivers; for other waters are ever flowing on to you." Similarly, every organization is always in flux—and always incomplete, unfinished, and only partially understood. The paradox is that change is bound up with continuity since most organizational problems can never be permanently "solved."[21]

Triangular design is *integrated* because no triangle is independent of the others. In *The Unbounded Mind*, Ian Mitroff and Harold Linstone posit *unbounded system thinking (UST)* as the most advanced of five inquiring systems and then argue that in this pattern, every aspect of a phenomenon or problem is related to every other aspect.[22] As noted earlier, (chapter 2, endnote 14), UST blends three perspectives—personal/individual, technical, and organizational/societal—that mirror, respectively, autonomy, control, and cooperation. Translating Mitroff and Linstone's claim into triangular design, every triangle is related to every other triangle.

Finally, triangular design is *sticky* because managers are embedded in those problems and dilemmas that are framed as triangular.[23] Stickiness runs counter to much of the current management literature, which encourages managers to behave as though they stand clearly and cleanly outside their problems. Thus does Henry Mintzberg inveigh against what he calls *thin management*, especially when it comes to strategy: "Portfolio management treats strategy as position, or at least a set of positions loosely coupled. That is compatible with thin management. But it is insufficient, because positions must have substance too; there must be some rich perspective behind each one. And such perspective cannot be developed without thick knowing, without deep-rooted involvement."[24]

In all, triangular design represents what Abraham Kaplan has termed *concatenated* theory, namely, "one whose component laws enter into a network of relations so as to constitute an identifiable configuration or pattern."[25] Kaplan contrasts such an approach with *hierarchical* theory, in which laws are deduced from a few fundamental principles. Organizations *are* concatenated, so that kind of theory fits.

THE FRACTAL CHARACTER OF TRIANGULAR DESIGN

As a nascent organizational "art form," triangular design can be described as not only concatenated but kaleidoscopic. My view has been stimulated in no small measure by exposure to the shapes of Buckminster Fuller, various tilings and tessellations, and the magical, interlocking figures of the Dutch graphic artist M.C. Escher.[26] Triangular design is also eminently *fractal.*

Fractal geometry refers to the seemingly "fractured" character of natural phenomena—which do not fit the perfect forms of Euclidean geometry. Chiefly the brainchild of mathematician Benoit Mandelbrot, fractal geometry recognizes that "Clouds are not spheres, mountains are not cones, coastlines are not circles, and bark is not smooth, nor does lightning travel in a straight line."[27]

Neither is measurement always what we take it to be. Mandelbrot asks rhetorically, "How long is the coast of Britain?" This question, he responds, is ultimately unanswerable because any measurement is based on an assumption of scale, and one can always select a different scale. In general, one can always choose a coarser or finer metric. Thus we have the paradox of infinity defined within apparently finite parameters.

For all its complexity, however, each fractal pattern is triadic—in a way that roughly corresponds to autonomy/control/cooperation. First, each fractal results from the reiteration of a simple *decision rule* (control). For instance, the Koch Snowflake (exhibit 7-1) is formed by adding to the middle of each side of an equilateral triangle another equilateral triangle with sides one-third those of the original—and then repeating this process again and again.

Exhibit 7-1

KOCH SNOWFLAKE
(First four orders)

Second, each fractal exhibits *self-similarity* (cooperation), that is, similar properties at different scales. Hence, all parts are of a piece, and the whole is visible everywhere. The parts "cooperate" graphically by forming mirror images of each other and microcosms of the whole.

Third, each fractal is a model of diversity and *increasing variety* (autonomy). Thus the Koch Snowflake mentioned above, after not too many iterations of the generative decision-rule, becomes complex enough to model even the most crannied of coastlines. Or consider the following portrait of the Sierpinski Triangle (exhibit 7-2),[28] whose embroidery develops *within* the initial triangle's boundaries:

Exhibit 7-2
SIERPINSKI TRIANGLE
(First four orders)

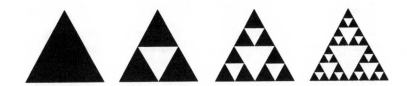

It was with fractal geometry prominently in mind that I developed the idealized Organizational Design Profile (exhibit 7-3, a reiteration of exhibit 3-9)—and then expressed this framework in an even more idealized Sierpinski-like graphic (exhibit 7-4) that summarizes chapters 4 through 6. The equivalent of a simple decision rule is the need to balance autonomy, control, and cooperation; the equivalent of self-similarity is the fact that every triangle evokes every other; and the equivalent of diversity is the increasing intricacy that results from repeating the balancing process at ever-finer levels.

And even though my core construct, an equilateral triangle, is Euclidean, virtually every triangle that I present is somewhat of a stretch and therefore imperfect—an approximation. Each triangle is indeed fractal—and reflective of "nature's relaxed geometry."

Exhibit 7-3

ORGANIZATIONAL DESIGN PROFILE

	AUTONOMY	CONTROL	COOPERATION
STRATEGY			
• **Constituencies** (For whose benefit does this organization exist?)	Customers/ clients	Shareholders/ subsidizers	Employees
• **Character** (What is our essential nature?)	Player-oriented	Coach-oriented	Team-oriented
• **Capabilities** (How do we compete?)	Differentiation (*special*)	Cost (*affordable*)	Flexibility (*adaptable*)
STRUCTURE			
• **Organization Chart** (What is the form of our reporting relations?)	Flat/clear	Steep/clear	Flat/amorphous
• **Layout** (What interaction does our physical design encourage?)	Independent action	Programmed interaction	Spontaneous interaction
• **Interdependence** (How does our work/ information flow?)	Pooled	Sequential	Reciprocal
SYSTEMS			
• **Reward System** (What behaviors are reinforced financially and nonfinancially?)	Individualistic	Hierarchic	Mutual
• **Meeting System** (For what reasons do people get together?)	Forum	Decision-making	Team-building
• **Decision System** (How do we exercise authority?)	Decentralized (*delegate*)	Centralized (*mandate*)	Shared (*collaborate*)

Exhibit 7-4

THE ORGANIZATIONAL DESIGN PROFILE AS A FRACTAL

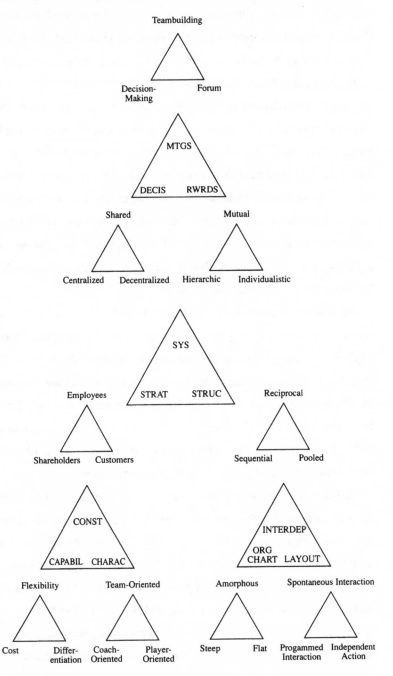

PRACTICAL GROUNDRULES

During the 1970s—with colleagues Eric Trist, John Eldred, Bill Whyte, Chris Meek, Stan Lundine, and others—I worked with the Jamestown (New York) Area Labor-Management Committee (JALMC) to try to help reverse a severe economic decline. JALMC was a multi-sector, multi-level undertaking that included a wide array of factory-level projects to increase productivity and improve the quality of working life. After several years' work, my colleagues and I speculated that although no single company had experienced systemic change, if all of the partial experiments that had been tried or were currently in progress were combined, the composite whole would simulate an organization undergoing systematic transformation. And indeed, that kind of effect was generated at the community level, in terms of a set of organizational change *themes*— such as skills development, layout redesign, and gainsharing—that became widely understood and adopted.[29]

My consulting experience with triangular design has been similar to that in Jamestown—if on a far more modest scale. Several clients have applied the concept and, to varying degrees, become fluent in triadic thinking. If all of the attempts to date were somehow formed into one, there would be at least the semblance of a systematic program. From these real-world clinical projects, and after extended reflection, I have induced three principles for applying triangular design. Each is illustrated by triangles created by (or with) client organizations.

1. Think in Threes—and search for parallels with autonomy, control, and cooperation. If nothing else, this exercise will help to uncover blind spots in conceptualization; more ambitiously, it will open up fresh perspectives. Granted, there is always the danger of contrived similarities. But the downside of spurious comparisons is small next to the upside of imaginative connections that previously had not been visible; hence, even if there is only, say, a two-thirds overlap between a particular triad and autonomy/control/cooperation, the parallel may still be worth drawing.

The question that should be asked is, does the comparison add to insight? If so, use it; if not, discard or rethink it.

I am *not* suggesting that one should immediately try to triangulate any new organizational issue or concern. A more prudent approach is to take as wide a compass as possible—by describing, explaining, and imagining in an open-ended way—and only later patterning in terms of triangles. On certain occasions, however, the press of events may make it useful to triangulate rapidly.

A few years ago a client, a large retail chain, was about to embark on "restructuring." Unfortunately, certain managers perceived this initiative to be a linear exercise in which changing the organization chart would automatically improve financial performance. I diagrammed this perceived causal chain as follows (exhibit 7-5):

Exhibit 7-5

RESTRUCTURING AS A LINEAR PROCESS

With my assistance, client management development staff drew a *performance food chain* (exhibit 7-6) to demonstrate the process that had to occur in order for the company to achieve its financial targets. This graphic, a variation on what had been described as a *constituencies performance cycle* (exhibit 4-2), depicts a triangle within a triangle. *Organization* was conceptualized as a balance of individual competence (autonomy), formal structure (control), and teamwork (cooperation). An effective organization produces *customer satisfaction*, which in turn results in the desired *financial performance* (which leads to further investment in the organization).

Exhibit 7-6
PERFORMANCE FOOD CHAIN

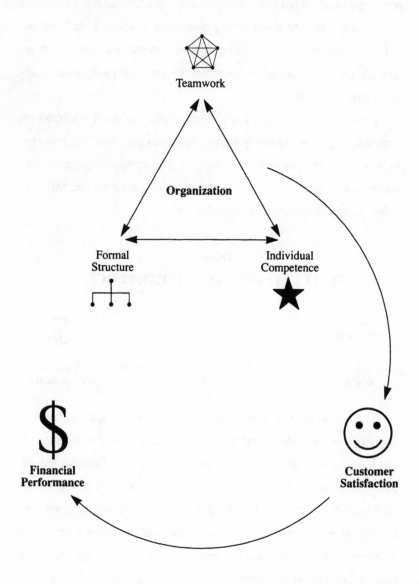

This image became a staple that unified a series of managerial team-building seminars across the company. In fact the *food chain* idea embodied three key properties of an organizational design pattern language: It was sensible, communicable, and portable. This representation was *sensible* because it revealed logical connections that everyone could grasp and verify as important. The representation was *communicable* in large part because it was a picture, with familiar icons,[30] that laid bare a complex set of dynamics. Finally, the representation was *portable* because its value was not dependent on any particular organizational setting or change program; managers could take the visual with them, wherever they might go within (and outside) the firm.

2. Play with Language. My main criterion for whether or not triangular design is "taking" within a client organization is the degree to which client members articulate their own triadic language—in expressions such as *performance food chain, manufacturing sweet spot,* and *triangular doughnut.* If the vocabulary has not become personalized, then the concepts have not become internalized. The best way to arrive at one's own language is to *play* with words—and graphics—in order to determine which expressions work—and fit.

One sure index of acceptance is humor. Exhibit 7-7—a spoof on an earlier version of my graphic depiction, "Decision Systems" (exhibit 6-5)—appeared throughout the World Bank more than two and one-half years after I had begun to work with the Bank's organizational planning staff as a consultant and an educator—a role that included conducting a Bank-wide seminar on decision-making patterns. An April 2, 1993 letter that I received from one of my colleagues/clients at the Bank is revealing:

I want you to know how triangular thinking is expressing itself in the organization. Yesterday, we got a copy of The Bank's Wordy (after the Bank's official internal rag, the Bank's Word), an annual publication put out every April 1. This would be the equivalent in the Bank of the skits done in a law firm at the expense of senior partners. It is probably the best read and the most anticipated publication within the Bank. We don't know who writes it, but they have an unerring flair for the topical. I attach a copy of a feature in the paper which will interest you and enrich your collection of triangles.

Exhibit 7-7
The WHY DECIDE Triangle[S&M]

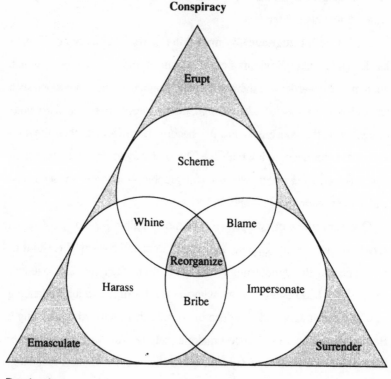

Bank's Wordy
The World Bank
Volume 9, Number 1
April 1993

Apropos of discovery and creativity, Cyril Stanley Smith argues that the ideal climate is one of relative freedom: "historically the first discovery of useful materials, machines, or processes has almost always been in the decorative arts, and was not done for a perceived practical purpose. Necessity is *not* the mother of invention—only of improvement. A man desperately in search of a weapon or food is in no mood for discovery; he can only exploit what is already known to exist. Discovery requires aesthetically motivated curiosity, not logic, for new things can acquire validity only by interaction in an environment that has yet to be."[31]

Smith goes on to detail the cornucopia of technologies that have issued from decorative uses, including metallurgy (from necklace beads, copper ornaments, and other jewelry), welding (joining bronze sculpture parts), ceramics (clay fertility figurines), minerals and compounds (pigments—including paintings on cave walls), horticulture (enjoyment of flowers), and animal husbandry (playing with pets).[32]

In light of this record, corporations that truly care about creativity would do well to build in some measure of slack. Thus Fred Kofman and Peter Senge recommend the value of a *practice field*—an offline setting in which people can play with ideas, confront otherwise-taboo topics, and generally open up their minds.[33] The opportunity to use a practice field can help individuals and groups make new connections—the third principle for applying triangular design.[34]

3. Connect, Connect, Connect. The secret to real estate is location, location, location. In show business, the trick is timing, timing, timing. In pattern-based organizational design, what matters is connection, connection, connection. Like the construction toy "K'NEX,"™ triangular design works best when one pattern—or triangle—begets another, which begets yet another, and so on. Eventually a tapestry develops.

A few "veteran" clients have developed their own unique catalogs of triangles. Johnson & Johnson's Barbara A. Marinan uses triangles as an organizing framework for a series of technical training programs and manuals.

On her own, she developed a coherent set of 57 triangles—now referred to as "Marinan's 57 Varieties"—that capture the essence of much pharmaceutical clinical R&D work. Exhibit 7-8, a five-level hierarchy relating to new-drug development, is taken from this set of 57.

Exhibit 7-8
TRIANGULATING NEW-DRUG DEVELOPMENT
(5 of 57 triangles)

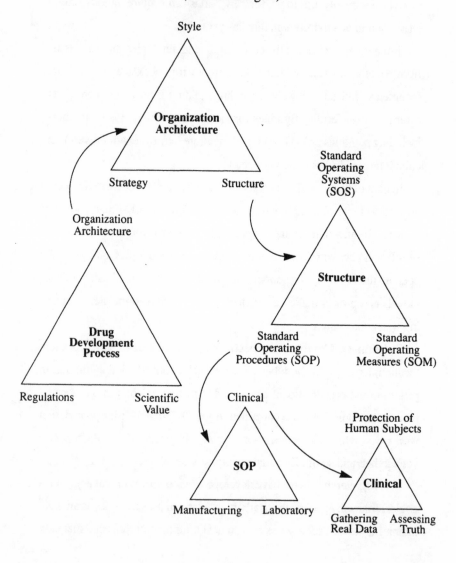

Note the very loose connection that these triangles have with autonomy, control, and cooperation. In fact, the links were drawn *after* the triads had been assembled—although it can be argued that they were subconsciously present all along. The point, however, is that such parallels—even if tenuous—provide an important measure of underlying structure.

One can ask in general: Is there an aspect of this (or of any given) issue that impinges on individual (unit) autonomy/diversity/independence? Control/uniformity/dependence? Cooperation/complementarity/interdependence? In my experience, most human-system issues contain some degree of all three aspects. And, at a minimum, the attempt at such a match—even if less than successful—deepens one's understanding.

The third principle for applying triangular design—"Connect, Connect, Connect"—is a metaphor for perhaps the most critical property of an organizational pattern language. If one theme runs through fractal geometry, natural science, and art/architectural/technological history, it is *connection*. Mathematician Ivar Ekeland has written, "From a strictly scientific point of view, there is only one thing we can apply the laws of physics to, and that is the universe. There is no physical subsystem which we could isolate from the influence of the rest of the cosmos."[35] Or as novelist E.M. Forster enjoins in *Howards End*, "Only connect!"

Yet connection can be overdone, to the point that confusion reigns. As Kevin Kelly has acknowledged, "We own the technology to connect everyone to everyone, but those of us who have tried living that way are finding that we are disconnecting to get anything done . . . . Connecting things is not difficult; the art is finding ways for them to connect in an organized, indirect, and limited way."[36]

Enter the autonomy/cooperation hybrid, an organizational pattern for tomorrow. Chapter 8 develops this model in the context of analogies and exemplars, as well as additional parallels from outside the field of organizational design.

C   H   A   P   T   E   R   8

A New
Organizational Form

"Many of us, or our successors, will hold regular jobs in
formal organizations with geographic identities and regularities,
with recognized clienteles and functions. . . .
But I believe such things will be routine, taken for granted,
unproblematic. Our preoccupations as a society, I believe, will not
be in this arena, but rather with what I have tried to designate as
complex organizations *of a much more fluid, ad hoc, flexible form.*
Perhaps these should not be designed organizations at all, and
the emphasis should instead be placed on the administration
of temporarily organized activities . . . with the development of
administration teams or cadres to specialize in a continuous process
of synthesizing. Perhaps complex organizations of the future
will be known not for their components but by their cadres,
with each cadre devoted to mobilizing and employing
resources in shifting configurations, to employ changing
technologies to meet changing demands."

—JAMES D. THOMPSON,
"SOCIETY'S FRONTIERS
FOR ORGANIZING ACTIVITIES" (1973)

121

The last twenty-some years have spawned a bewildering array of new organizational analogies that recall Thompson's vision. Although each entry has its own unique background, referents, and nuances, considerable overlap exists among these expressions. Most of the language about the "organization of the future" can be understood as a form of autonomy and/or cooperation.[1] In other words, emergent organizational patterns cluster along an axis between these two variables—and away from hierarchical control. Exhibit 8-1 illustrates this point (references are provided at the end of the chapter).

None of what follows is intended to discourage the generation of metaphors—especially those that are unlikely. I endorse wholeheartedly these words by John Van Maanen: "My sense is that the innova-

Exhibit 8-1
EMERGENT ORGANIZATIONAL FORMS
(References appear on pp. 140-42)

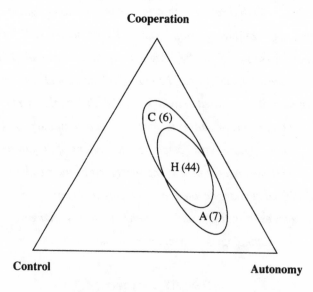

Cooperation

C (6)

H (44)

A (7)

Control   **Autonomy**

A: Autonomy bias
C: Cooperation bias
H: Autonomy/cooperation hybrid

Chronology:	H	Social pluralism/common ground (Emery & Trist, 1973)
	H	Systems structure = simulated decentalization/team organization (Drucker, 1974)
	H	Mosaic of subcultures (Alexander et al., 1977)
	H	Market-matrix organization (Miles & Snow, 1978)
	C	Adhocracy (Mintzberg, 1979)
	C	Circular organization (Ackoff, 1981)
	A	Atomized organization (Deal & Kennedy, 1982)
	C	Lattice organization (Gore Associates, 1982)
	H	Network/core group (McCaskey, 1982)
	H	Skunkworks (Peters & Waterman, 1982)
	H	Linked-dispersion model (Steele, 1983)
	H	Flexible specialization (Piore & Sabel, 1984)
	H	Baseball/basketball hybrid (Keidel, 1985)
	H	Networked teamwork (Keidel, 1985)
	H	New organizational form = autonomy/interrelationships (Porter, 1985)
	H	Network of commitments (Winograd & Flores, 1986)
	H	Collective entrepreneurialism (Reich, 1987)
	H	Third-wave company (Sculley, 1987)
	C	Transnational organization (Bartlett & Ghoshal, 1989)
	H	Federal organization (Handy, 1989)
	A	Shamrock organization (Handy, 1989)
	H	Network culture (Bolter, 1991)
	C	Cluster organization (Mills, 1991)
	A	Uncommon partnership (Banc One, 1992)
	H	Virtual corporation (Davidow & Malone, 1992)
	H	Alliance capitalism (Gerlach, 1992)
	A	Infinitely flat organization (Quinn, 1992)
	A	Inverted organization (Quinn, 1992)
	C	Spider's web organization (Quinn, 1992)
	H	Starburst organization (Quinn, 1992)
	H	Cave and commons design (Apple Computer, 1993)
	H	Horizontal corporation (Byrne, 1993)
	H	Managed disorder (Chiron Corporation, 1993)
	H	Compassionate capitalism (DeVos, 1993)
	H	Pizza organization (Eastman Chemical, 1993)
	H	Collaboratory (Heilmeier, 1993)
	H	Collaborative individualism (Limerick & Cunnington, 1993)
	H	Teamnet (Lipnack & Stamps, 1993)
	H	Connected isolation (Mayne, 1993)
	A	Spider plant organization (Morgan, 1993)
	H	Community without propinquity (Patterson, 1993)
	H	Free intraprise (Pinchot & Pinchot, 1993)
	H	Virtual community (Rheingold, 1993)
	H	Federation of entrepreneurs (Rodgers et al., 1993)
	H	Virtual co-location (Telnack, 1993)
	A	Modular corporation (Tully, 1993)
	H	Fractal company (Warnecke, 1993)
	H	Post-job organization (Bridges, 1994)
	H	Community of activists (Hamel & Prahalad, 1994)
	H	Fishnet organization (Johansen & Swigart, 1994)
	H	Society of work centers (Kelly, 1994)
	H	Electronic keiretsu (Manzi, 1994)
	H	Spherical organization (Miles & Snow, 1994)
	H	Coopetition (Noorda, 1994)
	H	Molecular organization (Ross & Kay, 1994)
	H	Blueberry pancake organization (Tyabji, 1994)
	H	Lean enterprise (Womack & Jones, 1994)

tive, charged work almost always comes from the margins. If the margins are drawn in—as they are in the American versions of economics—the good work looks elsewhere for a home. One of the attractions for me of organizational studies has always been its permeable boundaries."[2] Yet there is always a tension between newness on the one hand, and integration with what is already known on the other. Fresh organizational metaphors deserve consideration in their own right, but also need to be referenced to competing concepts and language. The concern of this chapter is with such integration.

The units of analysis covered by the autonomy/cooperation combination range from the small group (the "linked-dispersion" and "cave and commons" models of a management team's offices—in which private rooms intersect a shared space) to society as a whole ("social pluralism/common ground" and "collective entrepreneurialism"). Between these extremes lie such concepts as "lean enterprise," in which the counterpoint to control is explicit: "A concerted effort by companies across the industrial landscape to embrace the lean enterprise *and* find new tasks for excess employees will be vastly superior to any industrial policy that governments devise."[3]

Or consider W.L. Gore & Associates' "lattice organization," a term meant to convey the fact that "every individual within it deals directly with every other, one on one, in relationships best described as a cross-hatching of horizontal and vertical lines."[4] According to the late Bill Gore, who founded the company, "We don't manage people here. People manage themselves. We organize ourselves around voluntary commitments. There is a fundamental difference in philosophy between a commitment and a command."[5]

Of the 57 metaphors, 39 have appeared since 1989, and 27 of these surfaced in 1993–94; all but two of the latter parallel the autonomy/cooperation hybrid. Moreover, increasingly we find practicing managers and their organizations inventing language to characterize a new reality—such as Heilmeier (Bellcore)'s "collaboratory"; Chrio Corporation's "managed disorder"; DeVos (Amway)'s "compassionate capitalism"; Rodgers (Cypress Semiconductor)'s "federation of entrepreneurs"; and Tyabji (VeriFone)'s "blueberry pancake organization."

The growing popularity of the word "virtual" is also striking. This adjective has been applied to the community (Rheingold), to the corporation (Davidow & Malone), and to physical arrangements within the corporation, in the form of "co-location" (Telnack).[6] Indeed, in use as well as meaning (not to mention sound), *virtual* is veritably replacing *vertical*. Given the relentless development of microprocessors, neural networks, massively parallel computing, and wireless communications, the need for both *vertical* integration and long-linked production processes continues to diminish. With this decline has come a corresponding compression of the hierarchy necessary to coordinate affairs.

In the past, steep pyramids were required to orchestrate extended, lock-step sequences of work activities; hierarchy and work flow were mirror images of each other, offset 90 degrees. Advanced information technology has reduced the need for such assembly-line patterns and, as a consequence, has rendered organizational hierarchy—and physical location—less important.[7] People themselves—individuals and small groups, supported by powerful but flexible information-processing tools—are increasingly becoming the building blocks of organization, as well as the agents of organizational control. Steve Jobs has poignantly described the advantages of the autonomy/cooperation hybrid in terms of computer-related learning potential:

> Let's say that—for the same amount of money that it takes
> to build the most powerful computer in the world—you could
> make 1,000 computers with one-thousandth the power and

put them in the hands of 1,000 creative people. You'll get
more out of doing that than out of having one person use the
most powerful computer in the world. Because people are
inherently creative. They will use tools in ways the toolmak-
ers never thought possible. And once a person figures out
how to do something with that tool, he or she can share it with
the other 999.[8]

External as well as internal organizational boundaries are increasingly difficult to draw—in no small measure because of technological
change. Thus, Lotus chief executive Jim Manzi has documented the
emergence in the United States of electronic *keiretsu* (a Japanese term
for inter-company cooperatives), and notes that none of these arrangements were consciously designed; rather, all emerged as a response to
new technological capability in the face of extreme competitive pressures.[9] In 1993 alone, more than 500 digital-technology-driven
alliances were formed among American companies involved in media,
computers, and/or communications.[10]

Abstractly, the autonomy/cooperation hybrid reflects the way that
human memory works. Cognitive scientist Donald Norman believes
that our organization of information should mimic the brain's ability to
make connections without recourse to any controlling logic. Norman
contrasts *retrieval by navigation* (a hierarchical, rule-based pattern)
with *retrieval by description*: "Our memories do *not* work by navigation. We do not follow simple paths through memory, aided by signs
and maps. No, we think of something, and voom! there we are. That
reminds us of something else, and voom! there we are. . . . We describe
what we care about (mentally, to ourselves), and the system works
with that. Any description."[11] Norman draws conclusions about information processing that apply equally to corporate design. He observes
that "Today there is still too much emphasis on rigid organizational

structures, often devised to save time, money, or equipment rather than to simplify the user's task."[12]

Yet quite apart from the terms cited in exhibit 8-1, actual evidence of the autonomy/cooperation hybrid is becoming increasingly visible. Sales organizations are combining peer pressure through public performance ratings or rankings (autonomy) with the sharing of new leads, product/market information, and competitive conditions (cooperation).[13] Similarly, organizational consultants often must sustain a competitive/collaborative (autonomy/cooperation) relationship with various peers—as they find themselves sometimes competing for clients or research funds, and at other times working closely together. The same pattern plays out at larger system levels in the form of corporate joint ventures. The core issues are always, what do we share, and what do we resolutely not share (in order to safeguard our autonomy)?

The relation between basic R&D and applied R&D represents still another, more sequential form of the autonomy/cooperation hybrid. Traditionally in the United States, the path from the first to the second has been describable as going from autonomy to cooperation. The Japanese government has effectively reversed this order: "Japan has learned . . . that winning technologies are not picked, they are created—chiefly by promoting 'pre-competitive cooperation' to develop technologies that will help everyone, then feeding them back to private research labs when the product competition starts."[14] In other words, cooperation first—and then autonomy.

If, as noted above, management-team offices are appropriately arranged as a symmetrical blend of autonomy and cooperation, so too are the relations among team members—especially at senior levels. According to authors David Bradford and Allan Cohen, "The challenge for groups at the top is learning to both confront and support one another, maximizing individual contributions *and* collaboration."[15]

Finally, consider architecture and the shape of corporate (and other) buildings. Jonathan Hale equates height and hierarchy: "There may be a limit to how great a skyscraper can be, because the primary purpose of the skyscraper is to express corporate power. . . . The metaphysical cathedrals were much more down to earth than the skyscrapers of our time. It may be that the only buildings that should be as big as skyscrapers are buildings that reach out to everyone, buildings that embody the aspirations, the greatest dreams, of the whole community."[16]

The root logic for the autonomy/cooperation hybrid is the same logic that led Frank Lloyd Wright, in 1914–15, to design flexibility into Tokyo's Imperial Hotel: the need to cope with environmental turbulence. Wright knew that a rigid architecture would be shattered by an earthquake, so he created a building (for a marshy site) that could weather severe jolts: "He conceived a structure that, like a great ship, would float on segmented, massive concrete slabs supported on deep concrete pilings tied by flexible joints. Symmetrical and balanced, like a waiter's tray, it was to return to equilibrium after the shock wave."[17] (In 1923, Tokyo suffered its worst earthquake ever—8.1 on the Richter scale. Amid the rubble, the Imperial Hotel remained standing.)

EXAMPLES OF BLENDING AUTONOMY AND COOPERATION

There appear to be no limits to the constructive combination of autonomy and cooperation—whether at a micro or macro level, or anywhere between. Perhaps the best micro model is the professional service firm—in Tom Peters' opinion, a "pure 'knowledge play'" that is widely relevant because "*all* economic organization is fast becoming 'knowledge plays.'"[18]

A number of midsized companies—such as Herman Miller and Quad Graphics—fit the autonomy/cooperation pattern and have been widely chronicled by business writers. So does $21 billion-plus Hewlett-Packard, which on the one hand encourages units to cannibalize existing products (autonomy)[19] while, on the other hand, flexibly reassigns employees across divisions (cooperation)—thereby averting job losses.[20]

Here are thumbnail sketches of three other companies—vastly different and different-sized. Each organization, however, represents a conscious departure from strategies and behaviors based on hierarchical control. Coincidentally (?), each of the three is also vitally concerned with information, communication, and networking.

AT&T. Perhaps the largest-scale current effort to blend autonomy and cooperation is taking place at AT&T (1993 sales: $67.2 billion).[21] AT&T is trying to combine these variables up, down, and across the organization. At the top, two group structures have been established. The first is a Management Executive Committee responsible for strategy, policy, and values. The second structure is an eleven-person Operations Committee—made up of the chief financial officer and the group and regional heads—whose charter is "to ensure AT&T's operational success and profitable growth currently and in the future."[22] The chair of this committee changes each year, and members' annual bonuses reflect an even balance of their own business unit's performance and that of the corporation as a whole.

In the middle, each business unit has a dual charge: to perform well itself (autonomy) and to contribute to the larger enterprise (cooperation). Considerable resource-sharing takes place. To wit: "The AT&T Telemedia Personal Video System is a result of collaboration between our microelectronics, information systems and business equipment units. It brings together telephony and computing in a digital telephone and visual system that lets callers see one another in a window on their computer screens while they collaborate on documents."[23]

And at the bottom, AT&T is moving away from an adversarial, "line-of-scrimmage" labor relations posture that encourages the unions to dig in for job security. Instead, the company is collaborating with the Communications Workers of America and the International Brotherhood of Electrical Workers in crafting a model called "Workplace of the Future." AT&T is involving labor officials in corporate planning and is giving union members the opportunity to compete for jobs with offshore sites. Thus, an AT&T unit in Atlanta, by devising high-quality, low-cost production methods, won back communication refurbishing work that had previously been carried out in Matamoros, Mexico.[24]

AT&T's shift in labor relations is summed up by Harold Burlingame, senior vice-president for human resources: "We used to say, 'come here for a job for life.' Today we say, 'invest in us, we'll invest in you. . . .'"[25] On another occasion he added, "Career opportunities come as we address the market together."[26] (Throughout the company as a whole, the annual investment in continuing education, training, and development now averages more than $3,000 per employee.)

Moreover, AT&T has developed "Resource Link"—an internal quasi-employment agency that simultaneously expands individuals' job options throughout the company and promotes collaboration across business units. According to Douglas Merchant and Ruthann Prange, Resource Link "creates a web of interpersonal relationships that span unit boundaries—a sort of corporate neural network—increasing the cohesion and continuity of the AT&T community and giving people a broader perspective of AT&T's resources, needs, and opportunities."[27]

Computer Associates International, Inc. A compelling description of autonomy/cooperation is Hesh Kestin's account of software developer Computer Associates (CA) in *21st Century Management*. In the interest of brevity, here are two passages that capture the essence of the balance between the two:

Autonomy: Self-determined, measurable, and at the same time limitless, CA work is an amorphous endeavor whose success or failure may ultimately be gauged at the bottom line but, at the very same time, must always be judged against the relative success of the work of others, just as an individual baseball player's value is sometimes determined on such things as runs batted in but is always judged against the relative success of other players on the same team. Regardless of how it is measured, the value of the work of individuals is so important to CA that in sum it defies and ignores the twentieth-century credo that companies succeed or fail only because of decisions made in the penthouse. CA's culture of work—on the shop floor and everywhere else—is what makes CA work.[28]

Cooperation: Successful people in successful families establish a contract within the family. The terms and scope of such agreements may vary from situation to situation and change over time, but the essential element is a willingness to blend the personal ego into a greater ego, to desire and work for some greater good without compromising the dignity and integrity of the individual. In good families people work together—contractually.

The work contract at CA is rarely stated and is not written, nor need it be. Because the contract is not with the company—whose form keeps changing while the stationery stays the same—but with the people who hired you and those you hire—and those, assuming the constant reorganization that is the hallmark of CA, to whom you later report and who report to you.[29]

One could fill several pages with the aspects of this $2.1-billion company (1994 sales) that reflect autonomy and/or cooperation—

no small irony given the fact that most of the software CA writes is for the mainframe computer—a metaphor for control. But since founder and chairman Charles Wang plans to reduce mainframe business to 25 percent of CA's total by the end of the decade,[30] this organization may represent a test case from which IBM, Unisys, and other erstwhile mainframe mainstays can learn. According to Wang, "One thing that's special about CA is our speed. Everybody's always in motion. Where another company might make five decisions and get four of them right, we'll make fifteen and get twelve right. The percentages are the same, but we get more done because we don't let [politics] get in the way."[31]

And CA takes particular pains to ensure that its software will work both with products from other companies and with its own future offerings—as revealed by its perspective on software architecture: "By making the various software layers modular, connectable, Lego-like, we at CA can quickly and efficiently develop software for the fullest range of computers and operating systems. When new ideas come along, our clients know CA will make these work with their existing systems."[32]

Berrett-Koehler Publishers, Inc. Steven Piersanti, former president of Jossey-Bass and the founder of Berrett-Koehler Publishers, was less than enthusiastic about my including his firm as a model of autonomy/cooperation. Steve is a modest man to begin with, and his organization had already been widely profiled in the business press. Moreover, a favorable portrait of Berrett-Koehler within a BK book would almost certainly come off as self-serving. Still, his creation is such a powerful example of the new blend that I persisted, and Steve eventually consented.

In his introduction to Berrett-Koehler's Fall 1993 catalog, Piersanti reaffirms the plan behind BK's launch in 1992: "to create a new kind of publishing business based on partnership with our authors, suppliers and contractors, employees, customers, and societal and environmental communities. Our guiding concept was that each of these groups contributes to the success of a publishing venture; each is a 'stakeholder' in that venture; and thus our relationship with each should be more equitable, open, and participative than is typically the case in the increasingly 'lean and mean' world of corporate publishing."

Berrett-Koehler implements this vision in a host of ways. Here are just some of the commitments that the firm has made:

▲ The author has the right to terminate the publishing contract if for any reason he or she is not satisfied with either the publisher's performance or the overall relationship with the publisher.

▲ The author has considerable say in publishing details—including book cover design, interior format, and sales/marketing.

▲ The copyright is held in the author's name (instead of the publisher's, which is common practice among professional publishers).

▲ Author royalty rates go up to 20 percent of net receipts—a figure higher than that in nearly all other publishing agreements.

▲ The author has the right of approval over most subsidiary rights sales.

▲ The common clause that the publisher will have first-refusal rights to the author's next book has been deleted.

▲ There is no competing works clause that prohibits the author from publishing another work with a competing publisher that may conflict with the Berrett-Koehler book.

▲ Major stakeholders—authors, employees, suppliers, major customers, and communities—split 50 percent of the firm's pretax profits.

In all, Berrett-Koehler lives the values that it espouses and that it seeks in prospective authors and book projects. This firm is a structural model of what Piersanti, in an early concept piece, calls "a consortium or network of businesses that is more attuned than large corporate publishing to the technologies, organizational forms, and workforce values and motivations of our times." One practical consequence of this design is that authors interact fluidly with a wide array of BK staff and affiliates—from editorial, production, sales, marketing, and other offices. As I can attest, working as an author with Berrett-Koehler requires more independent and interdependent behavior—and concomitantly less dependence—than is the case with more traditional publishers.

Lest one think for a moment that control is unimportant at AT&T, Computer Associates, and Berrett-Koehler, consider these facts. Between January 1984 (when the "Baby Bells" were divested) and January 1994, AT&T reduced its workforce by 29 percent (from 435,000 to 308,700). This figure actually understates the extent of restructuring since one-fifth of AT&T's early-1994 complement came from mergers or new hirings during the previous five years.

Computer Associates, according to Kestin, "is a company where they physically lock up the seven-and-a-half-cent ballpoints nobody wants to use, much less take home; where paper clips are a line item in someone's budget; where you can get a computer, even two or three if you need them, but don't expect to find a mine of Post-it notes to decorate the screens."[33]

For its part, Berrett-Koehler has worked diligently to ensure a "strong, deeply ingrained, well-thought-out cash flow, low overhead, and a very sound cost structure." In addition, Berrett-Koehler exercises extraordinary discipline in selecting manuscripts for publication. Although the firm receives over 500 book proposals each year, it limits its list to about fifteen new titles annually.

THE NEW ORGANIZATIONAL FORM IN PERSPECTIVE

The autonomy/cooperation hybrid clearly is not for everybody. As non-American critics have legitimately pointed out during seminars I have led, this organizational blend makes little sense for the majority of struggling enterprises in third-world and other undeveloped countries. Then there is the national example of Singapore, which appears to be living a control philosophy quite successfully. Author Francis Fukuyama has argued that its "soft authoritarianism is the one potential competitor to Western liberal democracy, and its strength and legitimacy is [sic] growing daily."[34] Singapore may well test the limits of a control philosophy in a turbulent environment—especially to the extent that its citizens continue to prosper, and at the same time increasingly seek new liberties.

Neither does the autonomy/cooperation model fit the needs of commodity producers or service providers—or, for that matter, most manufacturing-intensive and process engineering-intensive corporations. Recall the control-biased *solution space* (exhibit 3-3), *manufacturing sweet spot* (exhibit 3-4), and *process engineering organizational options* (exhibit 3-5). Indeed, there will doubtless continue to be effective examples of organizational design that fit each viable area of the Organizational Design Triangle, as indicated by *generic organizational designs* (exhibit 3-1). (One wonders how many contemporary organizations are trying to force-fit themselves into a "horizontal," process-based design—a la the tenets of "reengineering"—that is both inimical to their culture and irrelevant to their competitiveness.)

But I believe that almost every society and organization will face intensifying pressures to support individual autonomy and spontaneous cooperation. Societally, as Arthur Okun pointed out (and as Charles Handy has reiterated), we will need both Adam Smith's *invisible hand* and an *invisible handshake.*[35] Organizationally, the challenge is simultaneously to appreciate and to integrate the demands of multiple stakeholders. To the extent that human systems meet such pressures, their behavior will come to parallel tendencies in both art and science. Or, put differently, social organization will resemble both conceptual organization and natural/physical organization.

Christopher Alexander ventures that 21st century art will parallel, in structure and excitement (if not literally), the brilliance of 14th and 15th century Turkish carpets. As discussed in chapter 7, such carpets achieve a sense of wholeness through a multiplicity of identifiable yet integrated *centers*: "The degree of wholeness which a carpet achieves is directly correlated to the number of centers which it contains. The more centers it has in it, the more powerful and deep its degree of wholeness."[36] Note the paradox here. The more "autonomy"—that is, the greater the number of freestanding building blocks or "centers" that a carpet exhibits—the more unity it also possesses. This is so because each center is a microcosm of the whole; it therefore complements, or "cooperates with," every other center and with the carpet as an entity. Indeed, the various centers of a complex carpet represent a multitude of different system levels—yet throughout the entire fabric, there is powerful integration. The pictures that Alexander presents and paints are holographic, even fractal. They are remarkably close to the images emerging from chaos theory and (especially) complexity theory.[37]

Philosopher Patricia Churchland provides a fitting introduction to complexity theory by observing that "Nature is not an intelligent engineer. . . . It doesn't start from scratch each time it wants to build a new system, but has to work with what's already there."[38] In other words, there is no overarching *control*. Rather, nature exhibits a dynamic interplay of *autonomy* and *cooperation*. According to complexity theorist John Holland, "the control of a complex adaptive system tends to be highly dispersed. There is no master neuron in the brain, for example, nor is there any master cell within a developing embryo. If there is to be any coherent behavior in the system, it has to arise from *competition and cooperation among the agents themselves* [emphasis added]."[39]

In short, complexity theory argues that there is a third realm, *complexity*, or the "edge of chaos," that represents a transition state between *order* and *chaos*. Chris Langton elaborates: "The science of Complexity teaches us that the complexity we see in the world is the result of underlying simplicity, and this means two things. First, that you can view the simple systems that underlie it all as being creative. . . . And second, because simple systems generate complex patterns, we really do have a chance of understanding those patterns. We have a chance of finding simple models that explain the creativity we see."[40]

In terms of triangular design, complexity parallels cooperation, order parallels control, and chaos parallels autonomy. The really interesting ideas have to do with chaos and complexity. John Holland uses the weather to illustrate. Holland shows that even though we cannot predict the weather beyond about a week, we still have weather science because "prediction [the *how*, or dependence—control] isn't the essence of science. The essence is comprehension [the *what*, or independence—autonomy] and explanation [the *why*, or interdependence—cooperation]."[41]

We need to take the arts no less seriously than the sciences. In a deep sense, human creativity—in organizations and in life—is *discovery*. It is understanding, articulating, and connecting, perhaps in starkly new ways, what is already there. Thus it is not surprising that Christopher Alexander should find inspiration for 21st century art in 600-hundred-year-old Turkish carpets. Or that Barbara Braun should detect the influence of pre-Columbian art on modern-day ceramics (Paul Gauguin), sculpture (Henry Moore), architecture (Frank Lloyd Wright), murals (Diego Rivera), and constructivist art (Joaquin Torres-Garcia).[42] Or that social scientist Eric Trist should have uncovered, in 1949—in a style of underground coal mining that was common prior to World War II—the basis for the self-managing teams that are revolutionizing organizations in the 1990s.[43] It is noteworthy that Trist's seminal book, *Organizational Choice*, is subtitled, "the loss, re-discovery, & transformation of a work tradition."

Indeed, although the origins of systems thinking are typically located in theoretical writings from the 1940s,[44] consider the following discourse on Japanese pictorial art, by Ernest Fenollosa in 1891:

> When several things or parts, by being brought into juxtaposition, exert a mutual influence upon one another, such that each undergoes a change, and as the result of these simultaneous changes each becomes melted down, so to speak, as a new constituent of a new entity, we have synthesis. . . . Here the parts are not left behind; they persist altogether transfigured by the organic relation into which they have entered. Such a synthetic whole is never equal to the sum of all its parts; it is that plus the newly created substance which has been formed by their union. Such a whole we cannot analyze into its parts without utterly destroying it. Abstract one of the units, and the light which irradiated it is eclipsed; it is like a hand cut off, limp and lifeless.
>
> . . . A true synthetic whole cannot have a single part added or subtracted without destroying the peculiar character of its wholeness, without disturbing the perfect equilibrium of the mutual modifications. Thus such a synthetic whole is an individual, a separate entity, [with] a peculiar organic nature, an unchangeable possibility, a foreordained unit from all eternity. Now [the] Japanese feel that every case of artistic beauty is just such an individual synthesis.[45]

Tomorrow's effective leaders, managers, and organizations will comprehend their futures in ways that are anything but hierarchical and linear. They will be *pattern masters,* uncommonly able to grasp meaning. These individuals and social systems will *see into* complexity efficiently, but without trivializing the phenomena that they encounter. And they will be able to communicate their visions and aspirations so that others can share, extend, and recreate them. Such is a far more hopeful prospect than yesterday's penchant for fashion, fad, and fix.

REFERENCES FOR EXHIBIT 8-1

Ackoff, R.L. (1981). *Creating the Corporate Future*. New York: Wiley.

Alexander, C., Ishikawa, S., and Silverstein, M., with Jacobson, M.,
Fiksdahl-King, I., and Angel, S. (1977). *A Pattern Language*.
New York: Oxford.

Apple Computer. (1993). In J. Markoff, "Where the Cubicle Is Dead,"
The New York Times, April 25, 1993, F7.

Banc One. (1992). In "Mightier than its Parts," *The Economist*,
December 19, 1992, 76.

Bartlett, C.A., & Ghoshal, S. (1989). *Managing Across Borders*. Boston:
Harvard Business School Press.

Bolter, J.D. (1991). *Writing Space*. Hillsdale, NJ: Erlbaum.

Bridges, W. (1994). *JobShift*. Reading, MA: Addison-Wesley.

Byrne, J.A. (1993). "The Horizontal Corporation," *Business Week*,
December 20, 1993, 76-81.

Chiron Corporation. (1993). In L.M. Fisher, "A New Model for
Biotechnology," *The New York Times*, April 4, 1993, F5.

Davidow, W.H., and Malone, M.S. (1992). *The Virtual Corporation*.
New York: HarperBusiness.

Deal, T.E., & Kennedy, A.A. (1982). *Corporate Cultures*. Reading, MA:
Addison-Wesley.

DeVos, R. (1993). *Compassionate Capitalism*. New York: Dutton.

Drucker, P.F. (1974). *Management*. New York: Harper & Row.

Eastman Chemical. (1993). In J.A. Byrne, "The Horizontal Corporation,"
Business Week, December 20, 1993, 76-81.

Emery, F.E., and Trist, E.L. (1973). *Towards a Social Ecology*. London: Plenum.

Gerlach, M.L. (1992). *Alliance Capitalism*. Berkeley, CA: University of
California Press.

Gore Associates. (1982). In L. Rhodes, "The Un-Manager," *Inc.*,
August 1982, 34.

Hamel, G., and Prahalad, C.K. (1994). *Competing for the Future*.

Boston: Harvard Business School Press.

Handy, C. (1989). *The Age of Unreason*. Boston: Harvard
Business School Press.

Heilmeier, G.H. (1993). In Peter Coy, "Bellcore to its Owners:
Don't Hang up," *Business Week*, December 13, 1993, 108.

Johansen, R. and Swigart, R. (1994). *Upsizing the Individual in the
Downsized Organization*. Reading, MA: Addison-Wesley.

Keidel, R.W. (1985). *Game Plans*. New York: Dutton.

Kelly, K. (1994). *Out of Control*. Reading MA: Addison-Wesley.

Limerick, D., and Cunnington, B. (1993). *Managing the New
Organization*. San Francisco: Jossey-Bass.

Lipnack, J., and Stamps, J. (1993). *The TeamNet Factor*, Essex Junction,
VT: Oliver Wight.

Manzi, J. (1994). "Computer Keiretsu: Japanese Idea, U.S. Style," *The
New York Times*, February 6, 1994, F15.

Mayne, T. (1993). "Connected Isolation," in *Morphosis*. Architectural
Monographs No. 23, New York: St.Martin's.

McCaskey, M.B. (1982). *The Executive Challenge*. Marshfield, MA:
Pitman.

Miles, R.E., and Snow, C.C. (1978). *Organizational Strategy, Structure,
and Process*. New York: McGraw-Hill.

Miles, R.E., and Snow, C.C. (1994). *Fit, Failure, and The Hall of Fame*.
New York: Free Press.

Mills, D.Q. (1991). *Rebirth of the Corporation*. New York: Wiley.

Mintzberg, H. (1979). *The Structuring of Organizations*. Englewood
Cliffs, NJ: Prentice-Hall.

Morgan, G. (1993). *Imaginization*. Newbury Park, CA: Sage.

Noorda, R. (1994). In A. Deutschman, "The Managing Wisdom of High-
Tech Superstars," *Fortune*, October 17, 1994, 197–206.

Patterson, S. (1993). In J. Gleick, "The Telephone Transformed Into
Almost Everything," *The New York Times Magazine*, May 16,

1993, 64.

Peters, T.J., and Waterman, R.H., Jr. (1982). *In Search of Excellence.* New York: Harper & Row.

Pinchot, G., and Pinchot, E. (1993). *The End of Bureaucracy and the Rise of the Intelligent Organization.* San Francisco: Berrett-Koehler.

Piore, M.J., and Sabel, C.F. (1984). *The Second Industrial Divide.* New York: Basic Books.

Porter, M.E. (1985). *Competitive Advantage.* New York: Free Press.

Quinn, J.B. (1992). *Intelligent Enterprise.* New York: Free Press.

Reich, R.B. (1987). *Tales of a New America.* New York: Times Books.

Rheingold, H. (1993). *The Virtual Community.* Reading, MA: Addison-Wesley.

Rodgers, T.J., Taylor, W., and Foreman, R. (1993). *No Excuses Management.* New York: Currency Doubleday.

Ross, G., and Kay, M. (1994). *Toppling the Pyramids.* New York: Times Books.

Sculley, J., with Byrne, J.A. (1987). *Odyssey.* New York: Harper & Row.

Steele, F. (1983). "The Ecology of Executive Teams: A New View of the Top," *Organizational Dynamics*, Spring 1983, 65–78.

Telnack, J. (1993). In S. Sherman, "How to Bolster the Bottom Line," *Fortune*, Information Technology Special Report, Autumn 1993, 16.

Tully, S. (1993). "The Modular Corporation," *Fortune*, February 8, 1993, 106–14.

Tyabji, H. (1994). In T. Peters, "Whence Comes Innovation?" *Forbes ASAP*, August 29, 1994, 132.

Warnecke, H.J. (1993). *The Fractal Company.* Berlin: Springer-Verlag.

Winograd, T., and Flores, F. (1986). *Understanding Computers and Cognition.* Reading, MA: Addison–Wesley.

Womack, J.P., and Jones, D.T. (1994). "From Lean Production to the Lean Enterprise," *Harvard Business Review*, March-April 1994, 93–103.

Notes on Design Methods

"Design is an attempt to move beyond past errors.
Default is the implicit ratification of unacknowledged history."

—CALVIN PAVA,

MANAGING NEW OFFICE TECHNOLOGY

There are several processes for diagnosing/redesigning an organization, or organizational unit, using any of the nine dimensions in the
Organizational Design Profile (exhibits 3-9 and 7-3, and the contents
of chapters 4–6). Obvious methods include internal and external
polling—through focus groups, surveys, and so on—and benchmarking. Here are some additional suggestions for gathering information
and gaining insight.

Constituencies. Archival data can help here. Annual reports,
vision/mission statements, credos, behavioral principles, and the like
often provide clues as to the relative importance of various stakeholders.
At a minimum, such documents are valuable as a basis for discussion.

Character. I have found knowledgeable third-party responses useful—especially with respect to organizational units or teams. For

example, the director of organization development in one billion-dollar company graphically characterized the top six managers in his firm as shown in exhibit A-1.

Exhibit A-1
A DISCORDANT TOP-MANAGEMENT TEAM

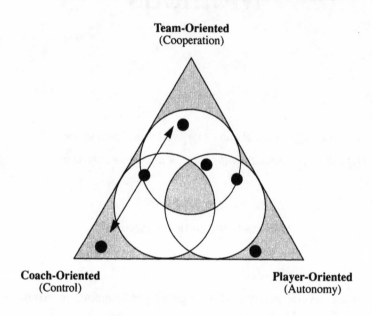

Team-Oriented
(Cooperation)

Coach-Oriented　　　　　　　　　　　　　　　　**Player-Oriented**
(Control)　　　　　　　　　　　　　　　　　　　　　(Autonomy)

Although some individual differences are clearly desirable, this degree of scatter precluded senior-management consensus on actual and desired organizational character. Three managers proved especially problematic—the two one-variable thinkers in the gray areas and a third individual who flip-flopped between control and cooperation, depending on what was politic at the time.

Capabilities. Customers/clients are often the best source of information on this dimension. Also helpful are consultants with significant industry/sector experience. Internal perceptions can likewise be valuable. In one retail firm, managers discussed the competitive strategies of other retail companies (including some from different industries) and then identified, in terms of the triangle, (1) the approximate location of each exemplar, (2) their own company's current location, and (3) their own desired location (see exhibit A-2).

Exhibit A-2

COMPARATIVE & SELF ANALYSIS BY "RETAILER"

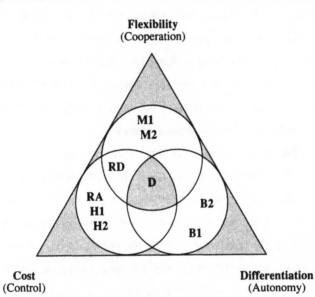

Flexibility
(Cooperation)

Cost
(Control)

Differentiation
(Autonomy)

B_1, B_2:	Boutiques (high-margin)
H_1, H_2:	Hyper stores (low-margin)
M_1, M_2:	Mini/convenience stores
D:	"Confused" department store
RA:	Retailer—actual
RD:	Retailer—desired

Organization Chart. Pictures of other corporate structures can help an organization gain perspective on its own pattern of reporting relations. As indicated at the beginning of chapter 5, copies of many companies' organization charts are available from commercial sources. Case studies and academic journals may also be useful; so, increasingly, is the popular press—in the form of both magazine articles and trade books. Exhibit 8-1 reveals the growing popularity of imagery as a substitute for (or supplement to) conventional boxes and lines.

Layout. People tend to team up with others who are physically accessible. As noted in chapter 5, vertical distance is especially likely to keep people apart (with two stories the equivalent of 300 horizontal feet, according to Christopher Alexander et al.). Therefore, the location of individuals who are collectively responsible for strategic decisions is critical. To determine who is appropriately positioned and who is not, one can conduct a simple "strategic interaction" analysis—a determination of who is (should be) talking with whom about key issues—and where these individuals reside.

Interdependence. Much "reengineering" has to do with reconfiguring work and/or information flow—interdependence. In terms of sharing information, electronic systems offer a functional alternative to physical layout: Since, in most cases, everyone cannot be in the same place at the same time, networking can link those who are physically distant. In terms of work flow, however, interdependence should match (or influence) people's physical location; in other words, work flow and layout should correspond. Toward this end, it is often useful to graph both the path of work and the physical configuration—and then reconcile these two patterns, if necessary.

Reward System. Obvious questions concern (1) the number of pay levels, (2) the ratios of top to middle to bottom pay levels, and (3) the nature and extent of participation in profit/gain-sharing or bonus/stock option schemes. Additionally, one might determine whether a particular unit or function or discipline appears to be in favor or disfavor. Comparative data are widely available from human resources/compensation consultants and trade associations. Moreover, the popular business press periodically reports on top-management compensation patterns.

Meeting System. Comparative data may be hard to come by in this area, but meetings that take place within a given organization are usually easy to inventory (technically, if not politically). The first step is to catalog all meetings, scheduled and unscheduled, that occur over a particular time period (for example, a month or quarter) and then to estimate the hours that each meeting consumes (perhaps by reconstructing history). The next step is to characterize each meeting in terms of the seven types indicated in the "Meeting Systems" triangle (exhibit 6-4). The final step—which will almost certainly have immediate change implications—is to summarize the amount of organizational time spent in appropriate and inappropriate meetings.[1]

Decision System. Comparative information on decision systems, like that on meeting systems, is difficult to obtain. The simplest way to describe an organization's decision system is to (1) identify the relevant players, (2) develop a list of the major decisions/decision areas for which that team is responsible, (3) review the different modes of decision-making presented in the "Decision Systems" triangle (exhibit 6-5), (4) match each decision with one of the ten modes of decision-making, and (5) characterize the overall decision-making pattern in terms of one or more of the ten modes.

A more systematic (and time-consuming) process—which verges on role analysis—is *responsibility charting.*[2] This technique uses a simplified vocabulary in order to describe each individual's part in each decision. After an overall decision/role matrix has been filled in, it is usually possible to map the dominant pattern(s) in terms of the triangular framework.

Static vs. Dynamic Portraits. Although the suggestions above provide snapshots, any or all such information can be represented as a motion picture—as was done with James River Graphics over a ten-year period (see exhibit 3-2). In this connection, it is important to bear in mind that any characterization is relative—to one's point of view, to other organizations, and to time. For example, General Electric over the past sixteen years has alternately been described as (1) autonomy-oriented, vis-a-vis "paternalistic" IBM (ca. 1980);[3] (2) autonomy-oriented under current CEO Jack Welch, vis-a-vis the "bureaucratic" organization that Welch inherited (in 1981);[4] and (3) "a tightly run ship that fosters high performance while maintaining rigorous controls," vis-a-vis GE's "free-wheeling" Kidder, Peabody & Co. subsidiary—an example of autonomy run amok (in 1994).[5] All three portraits may be valid; they simply represent different perspectives.

Theoretical
Triads

"Truth is much too complicated to allow
anything but approximations."

—JOHN VON NEUMANN, quoted in
MANFRED SCHROEDER, *FRACTALS, CHAOS, POWER LAWS*

Here are more than 200 triads—taken primarily from Western academic
and popular management and organizational literature (and secondarily from
writings on cognition and physical design)—that parallel autonomy/control/
cooperation. This list has been informally reviewed by various colleagues
and, in each case, subsequently shortened; it extends earlier catalogs (Keidel,
1985; 1987) but is by no means exhaustive. The citations represent three-
variable constructs that I have encountered in the course of teaching- and
consulting-related reading since 1982. A systematic search of the social science literature would probably yield many times this number of parallels.
Indeed, several of the works cited—such as Thompson (1967), Ackoff and
Emery (1972), Bartlett and Ghoshal (1989), Schrage (1990), Caine and
Caine (1991), Rhodes (1991), DePree (1992), and Kanter et al. (1992)—
include multiple triads that are not identified in this compilation.

Interestingly, the overwhelming majority of entries were not accompanied by a triangle or other graphic (such as a cube or three-ring Venn diagram). This general omission may reflect the relative absence of *visual* thinking even in otherwise holistic examples of Western organizational theory.

Let me put my argument in theoretical perspective. Thorngate's (1976) "postulate of commensurate complexity" posits that no theory of social behavior can be simultaneously *simple* and *general* and *accurate*. It can exhibit a significant degree of any one or two of these properties, but not all three (although it must display *some* measure of each). In terms of this postulate, the notion of *triangular design*—the need to balance three contrasting variables—is simple and general, but not highly accurate; it is a qualitative concept along the lines of Ouchi's (1981) "Theory Z," Deal and Kennedy's (1982) "corporate cultures," and Miller's (1990) "Icarus paradox."

Accordingly, the match of the following constructs with autonomy/ control/cooperation is uneven: Certain triads are closer in meaning to my framework than others. All entries, however, exhibit a degree of parallelism. The *shape* of this catalog is *relaxed* in the same way that, as noted in the text, Christopher Alexander refers to *nature's relaxed geometry*. Most triads are a variation on one or more of the three-way contrasts in exhibit B-1 (a restatement of exhibit 1-4).

My categories overlap, and many of the triads could be placed under two or more of these. In a few cases (such as Maslow [1943]; Greiner [1972]; Herbst [1976]; Mintzberg [1979]; Goldhar and Jelinek [1983]; and Maruyama [1992]), the triad I cite reflects the clustering of more than three variables. Moreover, different writers sometimes attach different meanings to the same word and/or use it in a different context; hence, certain terms appear in more than one column (e.g., *cognitive* appears under both autonomy [Mayer, 1992] and control [Janis, 1989]; *innovation* appears under both autonomy [Lawrence and Dyer, 1983] and cooperation [Broderick and Boudreau, 1992]; and *coordination* appears under both control [Beer and Walton, 1990] and cooperation [Kanter, Stein, and Jick, 1992]).

Exhibit B-1
SOME UNIVERSAL TRADEOFFS

AUTONOMY	CONTROL	COOPERATION
Environment	Systems	People
Natural/biological	Rational/analytical	Social/cultural
Discovery	Authority	Development
Identity	Method	Purpose
Freedom	Discipline	Sharing
Independence	Dependence	Interdependence
Uniqueness	Continuity	Reciprocity
Surprise/serendipity	Predictability/stability	Change/transition
Positives-increasing	Negatives-decreasing	Different
Product/market	Production/maintenance	Interaction/teamwork
Customer	Shareholder	Employee
Effectiveness	Efficiency	Intention
Differentiation	Cost	Flexibility
Separation	Subordination	Integration
Competition	Conflict	Collaboration
Behavior	Specification	Engagement
Bottom-up	Top-down	Lateral
Player	Coach	Team
Baseball	American football	Basketball
("Fill out the lineup card")	("Prepare the game plan")	("Influence the flow")

Finally, many of the triads do not reflect the main argument or structure of the works from which they are drawn. For instance, McWhinney's (1992) thesis is rooted in a 2x2 matrix, yet his concept of leadership styles is triangular *and fractal*—as diagrammed in exhibit B-2.

Despite all of the above qualifications, however, I believe that the following set of triads makes a persuasive theoretical case for understanding organizations as a balance of autonomy/control/cooperation. I should also note a parallel with the Tavistock Anthology, *The Social Engagement of Social Science*, edited by Trist and Murray (1990; 1993; forthcoming): Volumes 1, 2, and 3 are subtitled, respectively: the socio-*psychological* (autonomy), socio-*technical* (control), and socio-*ecological* (cooperation) perspectives.

Exhibit B-2

**TRIANGULATING McWHINNEY
(1992, 184-98) ON LEADERSHIP STYLES**

Integrative

Consultative   Participative

Pluralistic

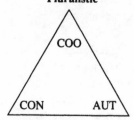

Authoritative   Charismatic

Task   **Facilitative**

Authoritarian   Expert   **Prophetic Entrepreneurial**

AUT: Autonomy
CON: Control
COO: Cooperation

WRITER	CONSTRUCT	AUTONOMY	CONTROL	COOPERATION

ORGANIZATION THEORY

WRITER	CONSTRUCT	AUTONOMY	CONTROL	COOPERATION
Perlmutter (1965)	Organizational types	Expendable organizations	Destructive organizations	Indispensable institutions
Boulding (1970)	System organizers	Exchange	Threat	Integration
Hirschman (1970)	Responses to decline	Exit	Loyalty	Voice
Ackoff (1974)	Organizing problems	Environmental-ization	Self-control	Humanization
Boulding (1978)	Spheres	Biosphere	Technosphere	Noosphere
Ouchi (1979, 1980)	Control mechanisms	Market	Bureaucracy	Clan
Pondy and Mitroff (1979)	Classes of system	Biological	Machine	Cultural
Schwartz and Ogilvy (1979)	Order-chaos relations	Anarchy	Hierarchy	Heterarchy
Keeley (1980)	Theoretical orientations	Biological analogy	Machine analogy	Social-contract analogy
Tuchman (1980)	Realms of man	Man at play	Man at war	Man at work
Scott (1981)	Organization as system	Natural	Rational	Open
Galbraith, J.K. (1983)	Instruments of power	Compensatory (exchange)	Condign (punishment)	Conditional (belief)
Grove (1983)	Modes of control	Free-market forces	Contractual obligations	Cultural values
Trist (1983)	Environmental forces rendering technocratic bureaucracies dysfunctional	Uncertainty	Complexity	Interdependence
Perlmutter (1984)	Social architecture paradigms for enterprise	Paradigm B (anti-industrial)	Paradigm A (industrial)	Paradigm C (social)
Gharajedaghi (1985)	Systems	Organic	Mechanistic	Social

WRITER	CONSTRUCT	AUTONOMY	CONTROL	COOPERATION
Kotter (1985)	States of complex social milieu	Diversity	Power dynamics	Interdependence
Carse (1986)	Boundaries of finite game	Space	Number	Time
Tzu (1988)	Three main facets of the warrior's art	The psychological	The physical	The social
Boulding (1989)	Faces of power	Economic	Threat	Integrative
Kilmann (1989)	World views	Open system	Simple machine	Complex hologram
Chandler (1990)	Patterns of capitalism	Competitive managerial	Personal	Cooperative managerial
Drucker (1990)	Societal sectors	Business	Government	Non-profit/ service
Schrage (1990)	Aspects of collaboration	Creativity	Media technology	Relationships
McGuire (1991)	Information states	Random	Ordered	Chaotic
Burt (1992)	Social structures of competition	Perfect competition	Monopoly	Network/ structural holes
de Bono (1992)	Stages of business	Stage 2: competition	Stage 1: production	Stage 3: integrated values
Lewin, R. (1992)	States of nature	Chaos	Order	Edge of chaos (complexity)
Waldrop (1992)	Transitions in dynamical systems	Chaos	Order	Complexity
Wheatley (1992)	Paradoxes of self-organizing systems	Renewal	Stability	Change
Drucker (1993)	Social climates	Capitalism	Marxism	Post-capitalist society
Galbraith, J.R., and Lawler (1993)	Replacements for bureaucratic control	Customer control	Automated formal controls	Peer control
Grove (1993)	Structural basis of computer industry	Personal computers	Mainframes	Networks
Toffler and Toffler (1993)	Three-level motherboard of global computer	Agrarian countries (leisurely "clock speed")	Industrial nations (faster than "clock speed")	Third-wave societies (hyper-speeds)

WRITER	CONSTRUCT	AUTONOMY	CONTROL	COOPERATION
Jackendoff (1994)	Concepts at basis of social understanding	Kinship	Dominance	Group membership
Kelly (1994)	Types of complexity necessary for vivisystem character	Open-ended evolution	Feedback loops	Distributed being
Roe (1994)	Alternative corporate structures	American	German	Japanese
Spencer (1994)	Organizational models	Organismic	Mechanistic	Cultural

STRATEGY/POLICY/PLANNING

WRITER	CONSTRUCT	AUTONOMY	CONTROL	COOPERATION
Mintzberg (1973)	Strategy-making modes	Entrepreneurial insight	Systematic planning	Ad hoc adaptation
Friend, Power, and Yewlett (1974)	Planning uncertainties	About operating environment	Of policy	About related choices
Trist (1976)	Planning philosophies	Disjointed incrementalism	Comprehensive planning	Adaptive planning
Porter, M.E. (1980, 1985)	Generic competitive strategies	Differentiation	Cost-leadership	Focus
Ackoff, Finnel, and Gharajedaghi (1983)	Planning postures	Reactive	Preactive	Interactive
Mintzberg and McHugh (1985)	Strategic forces	Divergence	Convergence	Alternating divergence and convergence
Coxe, Hartung, Hochberg, Lewis, Maister, Mattox, and Piven (1986)	Strategies for architecture firms	Strong idea	Strong delivery	Strong service
Nadler and Tushman (1988)	Strategic contingencies	Differentiation	Cost	Innovation
Bartlett and Ghoshal (1989)	Dominant strategic capabilities	Responsiveness	Efficiency	Transfer of knowledge and competencies

WRITER	CONSTRUCT	AUTONOMY	CONTROL	COOPERATION
Janis (1989)	Policy-making constraints	Egocentric	Cognitive	Affiliative
McDermott (1991)	Elements of USAA service recipe	Customers	Technology	Workforce
Broderick and Boudreau (1992)	Human resources competitive objectives	Quality/customer satisfaction	Cost leadership	Innovation
McKinsey Global Institute (1992)	Reasons for productivity differences in services	Openness to competition	Investment in high technology	Organization of labor
Pine (1992)	Ways to tailor products for mass markets	Create a new business	Move incrementally	Transform the business
Yearout and Hammond (1992)	Aspects of quality improvement	Quality as measured by customer expectations	Quality as a result of superior business processes	Employee involvement in quality
Bowman and Singh (1993)	Types of corporate restructuring	Portfolio	Financial	Organizational
Hronec (1993)	Categories of performance measure	Quality	Cost	Time
Maister (1993)	Kinds of professional-service project	Brains (expertise-based)	Procedure (efficiency-based)	Grey hair (experience-based)
Welch (1993)	Three most important things to measure in a business	Customer satisfaction	Cash flow	Employee satisfaction
Pfeffer (1994)	Approaches to achieving competitive success	Replacing people	Limiting scope of people's activities	Working with people

ORGANIZATIONAL DESIGN/STRUCTURE

WRITER	CONSTRUCT	AUTONOMY	CONTROL	COOPERATION
Miller, E.J. (1959)	Bases for differentiating operating systems	Territory	Technology	Time

WRITER	CONSTRUCT	AUTONOMY	CONTROL	COOPERATION
Woodward (1965)	Production systems	Unit	Mass	Process
Thompson (1967)	Patterns of interdependence	Pooled	Sequential	Reciprocal
Drucker (1973)	Ways of organizing work and task	Result-focused design	Work- & task-focused design	Relations-focused design
Galbraith, J.R. (1973)	Organization design strategies	Creation of self-contained tasks	Investment in vertical information systems	Creation of lateral relations
Segal (1974)	Types of organization	Mediatively structured	Chain-structured	Adaptively structured
Herbst (1976)	Types of group organization	Network	Bureaucratic hierarchical	Composite-autonomous; matrix
Henderson (1979)	Basic organizational form for complex operations	Decentralized operations	Centralized policy	Leadership which achieves consensus
Huseman and Alexander (1979)	Coordination alternatives	By feedback	By plan	By lateral interaction
Mintzberg (1979)	Coordinating mechanisms	Standardization of skills; standardization of outputs	Standardization of work; direct supervision	Mutual adjustment
Hersey and Blanchard (1982)	Fundamental types of control system	Enriched work	Assembly-line	Enlarged work
Peters and Waterman (1982)	Pillars of structure	Entrepreneurship	Stability	Breaking old habits
Goldhar and Jelinek (1983)	Manufacturing technologies	Independent tools and methods	Dedicated systems	Flexible systems; programmable systems
Lawrence and Dyer (1983)	Organizational readaptation outcomes	Innovation	Efficiency	Member involvement
Hrebiniak and Joyce (1984)	Contingency variables	Uncertainty	Complexity	Interdependence

WRITER	CONSTRUCT	AUTONOMY	CONTROL	COOPERATION
Keidel (1984, 1985)	Team sports metaphors	Baseball	Football	Basketball
Miller, D., and Friesen (1984)	Adaptive devices	Formal structural	Information processing	Interpersonal
Ouchi (1984)	Organizational types	H-form	U-form	M-form
Galbraith, J.R., and Kazanjian (1986)	Primary management challenges	Diversity	Globalization	Innovation
Chisholm (1989)	Origins of interdependence	Natural	Artificial	Voluntary
Hirschhorn (1989)	Balancing issues confronting professional organizations	Individual	Professional skills	Group life
Jaques (1989)	Basic concepts for designing requisite organization	Individual capability & maturation of human capability	Hierarchical pattern of organizational layers	Horizontal working relationships
Walton (1989)	Information technology implementation effectiveness ingredients	Strong competence	Good direction	High organizational commitment
Eisenhardt (1990)	Characteristics of effective decisions	High-quality	Strategic	Fast
Womack, Jones, and Roos (1990)	Types of Production	Craft	Mass	Lean
Ackoff (1991)	Obstructions imposed by bureaucracies	Ineffectiveness	Inefficiency	Inhumanity
Blaxill and Hout (1991)	Organizational types	Robust	Bureaucratic	Niche
Haspeslagh and Jemison (1991)	Acquisition integration approaches	Preservation	Absorption	Symbiosis

WRITER	CONSTRUCT	AUTONOMY	CONTROL	COOPERATION
Keen (1991)	Principles of information technology management education	Forum for dialogue	Education for action	Sustained commitment
Keidel (1991)	Organizing components that support corporate direction	Reward system	Authority structure	Interaction patterns
Conner (1993)	Post-merger/ acquisition relationships	Coexistence	Assimilation	Transformation
Frohman (1993)	Foci of management models	Personal initiative	Leaders' behavior	Organization structure
Hambrick (1993)	Types of multinational group tasks	Creative	Computational	Coordinative
Katzenbach and Smith (1993)	Team basics	Accountability	Skills	Commitment
Tomasko (1993)	Replacements for workers and their bosses	Reinforced jobs	Load-bearing managers	Composite teams
Womack and Jones (1994)	Needs that conflict with those of value stream	Individual	Functional	Company

PHYSICAL DESIGN/ARCHITECTURE/ART

WRITER	CONSTRUCT	AUTONOMY	CONTROL	COOPERATION
Dow (1899)	Elements of all visual arts	The picture	The plan	The process
Wright (1945)	Universal ideals embodied in Japanese art	Aesthetic wholeness	Functional honesty	Moral goodness
Jones (1967)	Criteria for designing, planning, and testing	Exploratory	Predictive	Flexible
Eisner (1972)	Orientations to teaching of art	Child-centered	Subject-centered	Society-centered
Sundstrom (1986)	Units of analysis in physical environment	Individual	Organizational	Interpersonal relationship

WRITER	CONSTRUCT	AUTONOMY	CONTROL	COOPERATION
Kappraff (1991)	Canons that underlie good architectural/artistic design	Variety	Repetition	Harmony
Jones (1992)	Stages of design process	Divergence (1)	Convergence (3)	Transformation (2)
Joskowicz, Williams, Cagan, and Dean (1993)	Stages of design process	Generate	Evaluate	Modify
Mitchell (1993)	Bases for designing	Geometrical criteria	Technological capability	People's experiences & actions
Nute (1993)	Geometric abstractions	Natural forms	Man-made forms	Social forms
Warnecke (1993)	Development path in engineering	Primitive (1)	Complicated (2)	Simple (3)
Hale (1994)	Concepts of a building	Nature	Imitation of nature	Expression of *our* nature

LEADERSHIP/MANAGEMENT/DECISION-MAKING

Belbin (1981)	Characteristics of ideal management team chairman	Delegation of work	Firmness of direction	Skill in consultation
Pascale and Athos (1981)	Executive triangle	Independent behavior	Dependent behavior	Interdependent behavior
Bradford and Cohen (1984)	Models of leadership	Manager-as-technician	Manager-as-conductor	Manager-as-developer
Shaw, M.E. (1984)	Leadership/ communication styles	Accommodating	Controlling	Developmental
Leavitt (1986)	Management phases	Pathfinding	Problem-solving	Implementing
Scholtes (1988)	Joiner triangle for organizational success criteria	Quality	Scientific approach	All one team
Vroom and Jago (1988)	Eras of management	Era of the craftsman (1)	Scientific management (2)	Participative management (3)

WRITER	CONSTRUCT	AUTONOMY	CONTROL	COOPERATION
Ancona and Nadler (1989)	Core processes of executive team effectiveness	External boundary management	Work management	Relationship management
d'Iribarne (1989)	Basic principles (*logiques*) of management	Fair contract	Class honor	Consensus
Mintzberg (1989)	Levels of decision-making in the professional organization	Professional judgment	Administrative fiat	Collective choice
Jonas, Fry, and Srivastva (1990)	Cornerstones of the executive task	Novelty	Continuity	Transition
Nye (1990)	Aspects of power	Economic	Military	Co-optive
Barzun (1991)	Ways to run a college or university	Student power	Central control	Principle of reciprocity
Chajet and Shachtman (1991)	Aspects of corporate leadership for image management	Vision	Oversight	Motivation
Dixit and Nalebuff (1991)	Components of interactive decision	Own choice	Conflict	Cooperation
Hirschhorn (1991)	Managerial roles in team environment	Individuals	Manager	Team
Levitt (1991)	Things that effective managers do	Thinking	Operating	Changing
Rhodes (1991)	Yardsticks for measuring the manager of the future	Market awareness	Conceptual power	Skill with people
Schwartz (1991)	Considerations in selecting scenario development team	Diversity	Top management involvement	Capacity to work as a team
Brownstein and Panner (1992)	Guidelines for corporate compensation committees	Establish independence	Articulate a mandate	Communicate to constituencies
DePree (1992)	Ideas at intersection of ethics and leadership	Celibacy	Justice	Common good

WRITER	CONSTRUCT	AUTONOMY	CONTROL	COOPERATION
Eccles and Nohria, with Berkley (1992)	Factors comprising essence of management	Identity	Action	Rhetoric
Etzioni (1992)	Factors that account for variances in decision-making	Individual	Structural	Cultural
Kaplan and Norton (1992)	Sets of operational measures	Customer satisfaction	Internal processes	Organization's ability to learn & improve
Kotter and Heskett (1992)	Key corporate constituencies	Customers	Shareholders	Employees
McWhinney (1992)	Leadership styles	Charismatic	Authoritative	Pluralistic
Thomas (1992)	Decision-making models	Garbage can	Rational	Political
Block (1993)	Challenges of governance	Learning to adapt to customers & marketplace	Doing more with less	Creating passion & commitment in employees
Kahn and Kram (1994)	Internal models of authority	Counterdependent	Dependent	Interdependent
Wills (1994)	Authority bases of leadership	Charismatic	Traditional	Legalistic

STYLE/CULTURE

WRITER	CONSTRUCT	AUTONOMY	CONTROL	COOPERATION
Lewin, K. (1947)	Social climates	Laissez-faire	Autocracy	Democracy
Hall (1959)	Levels of culture	Formal	Technical	Informal
Etzioni (1961)	Control/ involvement	Utilitarian/ remunerative	Coercive/ alienative	Normative/ moral
Ansoff (1979)	Power processes	Bargaining	Coercive	Consensual
Smith, W.E., Lethem, and Thoolen (1980)	Types of power	Appreciation	Control	Influence

WRITER	CONSTRUCT	AUTONOMY	CONTROL	COOPERATION
Fisher and Ury (1981)	Criteria for judging method of negotiation	Production of wise agreement	Efficiency	Improved relationship between parties
Bennis and Nanus (1985)	Styles of social architecture	Personalistic	Formalistic	Collegial
Raelin (1985)	Streams of culture	Professional	Corporate	Social
Savage, Blair, and Sorenson (1989)	Negotiation tactics	Competitive	Subordinative	Collaborative
Gagliardi (1990)	Organizational artifacts	Natural	Artificial	Socially constructed
Sheridan (1992)	Organizational cultural values	Individual	Work task	Interpersonal relationship

DEVELOPMENT/CHANGE/INNOVATION

WRITER	CONSTRUCT	AUTONOMY	CONTROL	COOPERATION
Greiner (1972)	Organizational growth stages	Creativity; delegation	Direction; coordination	Collaboration
Abernathy and Utterback (1975)	Product/process innovation patterns	Fluid pattern	Specific pattern	Transitional pattern
Beer (1980)	Approaches to change	Bottom-up	Top-down	Shared responsibility
Keidel (1982)	Quality of working life development trajectories	Induced	Planned	Evolved
Oshry (1986)	Organizational possibilities	Mutual understanding & accommodation	Internal warfare	Transformation
Lawler (1988)	Approaches to change	Track-2: network	Track-1: traditional	Track-3: high-involvement
Stata (1989)	Types of innovation	Product	Process	Management
Beer, Eisenstat, and Spector (1990)	Roles of corporate human resource professionals in effective revitalizations	Serving as coaches	Aiding in planning & monitoring	Facilitating sharing of learning

WRITER	CONSTRUCT	AUTONOMY	CONTROL	COOPERATION
Beer and Walton (1990)	Objectives of organization development	Competence	Coordination	Commitment
Bookchin (1990)	Aspects of human development	Freedom	Rationality	Society
Bell (1991)	Prerequisites for empowerment	Payoff	Proficiency	Purpose
Tesler (1991)	Changes in role of computer	Personal implement (2)	Cloistered oracle (1)	Active assistant (3)
Beckhard and Pritchard (1992)	Aspects of fundamental change model	External forces	Business decisions	Organizational consequences
Kanter, Stein, and Jick (1992)	Forms of change	Identity	Control	Coordination
Modis (1992)	Aspects of evolution of innovation	Selection	Diffusion	Mutation
Prokop (1992)	Steps for starting an environmental management program	Assess existing habits within your organization	Reduce consumption unilaterally throughout the organization	Adopt an organization-wide policy for influencing others whenever possible
Weisbord (1992)	Essentials of search-conference design	Theories	Techniques	Values
Wheelwright and Clark (1992)	Competitive imperatives for development of new products and processes	Quality (products with distinction & integrity)	Efficiency (high development productivity)	Speed (fast & responsive)
Kohn (1993)	Three C's of quality	Content	Choice	Collaboration
Leo (1993)	Three-stage architecture of engagement for organizational learning	Finding those predisposed (stage 1)	Practical experiment- ation (stage 3)	Core community- building activities (stage 2)
Liu (1993)	Research issues prominent in perspective taking	Which perspectives to take	How to represent perspectives	When to shift from one perspective to another

WRITER	CONSTRUCT	AUTONOMY	CONTROL	COOPERATION
Blumenthal and Haspeslagh (1994)	Types of corporate transformation	Corporate self-renewal	Improving operations	Strategic transformation

INDIVIDUAL/INTERPERSONAL

WRITER	CONSTRUCT	AUTONOMY	CONTROL	COOPERATION
Maslow (1943)	Human needs	Self-actualization	Physiological, safety, & security	Belongingness, social, & love
Bion (1961)	Group assumptions	Fight/flight	Dependence	Pairing
McClelland (1962)	Learned needs	Achievement	Power	Affiliation
Wallen (1963)	Types of executive personality	Achiever	Critic	Helper
Ackoff and Emery (1972)	Purposes of communication	Information	Instruction	Motivation
Porter, E.H. (1973)	Patterns of motivation	Analytic-autonomizing	Assertive-directing	Altruistic-nurturing
Katz (1974)	Skills of an effective administrator	Conceptual	Technical	Human
Pirsig (1974)	Internal gumption traps	Truth (cognitive understanding)	Muscle (psycho-motor understanding)	Value (affective understanding)
Axelrod (1984)	Forms of social interaction	Noncooperation	Exploitation	Cooperation
Schein (1985)	Bases for structuring human relationships	Individuality/ competition	Lineality	Collaterality/ group cooperation
Schutz (1987)	Behavior vis-a-vis other people	Open to	Controlling of	Including of
Anthony, Maddox, and Wheatley (1988)	Self-efficacy triangle	Projective expectancies	Demonstrated skills	Realistic positive attitudes
Beggan (1989)	Types of people based on world view	Individualists	Competitors	Cooperators
DeLuca (1992)	Types of manager	Competitor	Turf builder	Team builder

165

WRITER	CONSTRUCT	AUTONOMY	CONTROL	COOPERATION
Maruyama (1992)	Mindscapes	I-type	H-type	S-type, G-type
Gerson (1993)	Men's roles vis-a-vis family	Autonomous men	Breadwinners	Involved fathers
Kiechel (1994)	Nature of managers' world	Changing possibilities	Changing technologies	Changing teams

INTELLIGENCE/THINKING/LEARNING/CREATIVITY

WRITER	CONSTRUCT	AUTONOMY	CONTROL	COOPERATION
Piaget (1974)	Psychological research tendencies concerning development of intelligence and cognitive structures	Innateness	Empiricism	Constructivism
MacLean (1978)	Brain "layers"	Neo-cortex	R-complex	Limbic system
Torrance (1979)	Aspects of creative behavior	Abilities	Skills	Motivations
Smith, C.S. (1982)	Man's means of manipulating new blocks of thought patterns	Preserving	Replicating	Communicating
Minsky (1985)	Components of an architecture of a mind society	Insulated systems	Distinct levels of management	Distributed systems
Jackendoff (1987)	Domains of psychology	Brain	Computational mind	Phenomenological mind
Amabile (1988)	Components of creative performance	Creativity-relevant skills	Domain-relevant skills	Task motivation
Maidique and Zirger (1988)	Dimensions of learning by moving away from home base	Newness of market	Newness of technology	Newness of organization
Sternberg (1988)	Basic elements of mental self-management	Selecting new environments	Adapting to environments	Shaping environments
Academy of Management (1990)	Elements of credo	Discovering managerial knowledge	Applying managerial knowledge	Sharing managerial knowledge

WRITER	CONSTRUCT	AUTONOMY	CONTROL	COOPERATION
Seligman (1990)	Dimensions of explanation	Personalization	Permanence	Pervasiveness
Caine and Caine (1991)	Higher-order thinking skills	Discovering unique solutions	Analysis	Synthesis
Hofstede (1991)	Levels of uniqueness in human mental programming	Personality (specific to individual)	Human nature (universal)	Culture (specific to group or category)
Basadur (1992)	Components of creative activity in an organization	Problem finding	Problem solving	Solution implementation
Holland (1992)	Aspects of (artificial) intelligence	Competition	Consistency	Cooperation
Kosslyn and Koenig (1992)	Cognitive neuroscience triangle	Brain	Computation	Behavior
Mayer (1992)	Aspects of thinking	Cognitive	Directed	Process
Shaw, R.B., and Perkins (1992)	Barriers to organizational learning	Insufficient capacity to reflect	Insufficient capacity to act	Insufficient capacity to disseminate
Mitroff and Linstone (1993)	Multiple perspectives of unbounded systems thinking	Personal	Technical	Organizational
Rand (1993)	Sources of knowing	Intuition	Programming	Intention
Schein (1993)	Types of learning	Knowledge acquisition and insight	Habit and skill learning	Emotional conditioning and learned anxiety
Weick and Roberts (1993)	Actors' actions necessary for collective mind	Contributions	Subordination	Representation

REFERENCES

Abernathy, W.J., and Utterback, J. (1975). "A Dynamic Model of Product and Process Innovation." *Omega, 3* (6), 639-57.

Academy of Management (1990). "The Academy of Management Code of Ethical Conduct—Credo," *Academy of Management Journal, 33* (4), 901.

Ackoff, R.L. (1974). *Redesigning the Future.* New York: Wiley.

Ackoff, R.L. (1991). *Ackoff's Fables.* New York: Wiley.

Ackoff, R.L., and Emery, F.E. (1972). *On Purposeful Systems.* Chicago: Aldine-Atherton.

Ackoff, R.L., Finnel, E.V., and Gharajedaghi, J. (1983). *A Guide to Controlling Your Own Corporation's Future.* New York: Wiley.

Amabile, T.M. (1988). "From Individual Creativity to Organizational Innovation." In K. Gronhaud and G. Kaufmann (eds.), *Innovation.* Universitetsforlaget, Norway: Norwegian University Press (distributed by Oxford University Press), 139-66.

Ancona, D.G., and Nadler, D.A. (1989). "Top Hats and Executive Tales: Designing the Senior Team." *Sloan Management Review,* Fall 1989, 19-28.

Ansoff, H.I. (1979). *Strategic Management.* London: Macmillan.

Anthony, W.P., Maddox, E.N., and Wheatley, W., Jr. (1988). *Envisionary Management.* New York: Quorum Books.

Axelrod, R. (1984). *The Evolution of Cooperation.* New York: Basic Books.

Bartlett, C.A., and Ghoshal, S. (1989). *Managing Across Borders.* Cambridge, MA: Harvard Business School Press.

Barzun, J. (1991). *Begin Here.* Chicago: University of Chicago Press.

Basadur, M. (1992). "Managing Creativity: A Japanese Model." *Academy of Management Executive,* May 1992, 29-42.

Beckhard, R., and Pritchard, W. (1992). *Changing The Essence.* San Francisco: Jossey-Bass.

Beer, M. (1980). *Organization Change and Development.* Glenview, IL: Scott, Foresman.

Beer, M., Eisenstat, R.A., and Spector, B. (1990). *The Critical Path to Corporate Renewal.* Boston: Harvard Business School Press.

Beer, M., and Walton, E. (1990). "Developing the Competitive Organization: Interventions and Strategies," *American Psychologist, 45* (2), 154-61.

Beggan, J. (1989). "Cooperators, Competitors and Individualists," *Boardroom Reports*, June 15, 1989, 14.

Belbin, M. (1981). *Management Teams.* New York: Wiley.

Bell, C.R. (1991). "Empowerment is Not a Gift." *Training*, December 1991, 98.

Bennis, W., and Nanus, B. (1985). *Leaders.* New York: Harper & Row.

Bion, W.R. (1961). *Experiences in Groups.* London: Tavistock.

Blaxill, M.F., and Hout, T.M. (1991). "The Fallacy of the Overhead Quick Fix," *Harvard Business Review*, July-August 1991, 93-101.

Block, P. (1993). *Stewardship.* San Francisco: Berrett-Koehler.

Blumenthal, B., and Haspeslagh, P. (1994). "Toward a Definition of Corporate Transformation," *Sloan Management Review*, Spring 1994, 101-06.

Bookchin, M. (1990). *Remaking Society.* Boston: South End Press.

Boulding, K.E. (1970). *Beyond Economics.* Ann Arbor, MI: Ann Arbor Paperbacks.

Boulding, K.E. (1978). *Ecodynamics.* Beverly Hills, CA: Sage.

Boulding, K.E. (1989). *Three Faces of Power.* Newbury Park, CA: Sage.

Bowman, E.H., and Singh, H. (1993)."Corporate Restructuring: Reconfiguring the Firm," *Strategic Management Journal*, Summer 1993 Special Issue, *14* (1-3), 5-14.

Bradford, D.L., and Cohen, A.R. (1984). *Managing for Excellence.* New York: Wiley.

Broderick, R., and Boudreau, J.W. (1992). "Human Resource Management, Information Technology and the Competitive Edge." *Academy of Management Executive*, May 1992, 7-17.

Brownstein, A.R., and Panner, M.J. (1992). "Who Should Set CEO Pay? The Press? Congress? Shareholders?" *Harvard Business Review*, May-June 1992, 28-38.

Burt, R.S. (1992). *Structural Holes.* Boston: Harvard University Press.

Caine, R.N., and Caine, G. (1991). *Making Connections.* Alexandria, VA: Association for Supervision and Curriculum Development.

Carse, J.P. (1986). *Finite and Infinite Games.* New York: Ballantine Books.

Chajet, C., and Shachtman, T. (1991). *Image by Design.* Reading, MA: Addison-Wesley.

Chandler, A.D. (1990). *Scale and Scope*. Boston: Harvard University Press.

Chisholm, D. (1989). *Coordination Without Hierarchy*. Berkeley: University of California Press.

Conner, D.R. (1993). *Managing at the Speed of Change*. New York: Villard Books.

Coxe, W., Hartung, N.F., Hochberg, H.H., Lewis, B.J., Maister, D.H., Mattox, R.F., and Piven, P.A. (1986). "Charting Your Course," *Architectural Technology*, May/June 1986, 52-58.

Deal, T.E., and Kennedy, A.A. (1982). *Corporate Cultures*. Reading, MA: Addison-Wesley.

de Bono, E. (1992). *Sur/petition*. New York: HarperBusiness.

DeLuca, J.M. (1992). *Political Savvy*. Horsham, PA: LRP Publications.

DePree, M. (1992). *Leadership Jazz*. New York: Currency Doubleday.

d'Iribarne, P. (1989). Cited in G. Hofstede, "Cultural Constraints in Management Theories," *Academy of Management Executive*, February 1993, 81-94.

Dixit, A.K., and Nalebuff, B.J. (1991). *Thinking Strategically*. New York: Norton.

Dow, A.W. (1899). *Composition*. Boston: J.M. Bowles.

Drucker, P.F. (1973). *Management*. New York: Harper and Row.

Drucker, P.F. (1990). *Managing the Nonprofit Organization*. New York: HarperCollins.

Drucker, P.F. (1993). *Post-Capitalist Society*. New York: HarperBusiness.

Eccles, R.G., and Nohria, N., with Berkley, J.D. (1992). *Beyond the Hype*. Boston: Harvard Business School Press.

Eisenhardt, K.M. (1990). "Speed and Strategic Choice: How Managers Accelerate Decision Making." *California Management Review*, Spring 1990, 39-54.

Eisner, E.W. (1972). *Educating Artistic Vision*. New York: Macmillan.

Etzioni, A. (1961). *A Comparative Analysis of Complex Organizations*. New York: Free Press.

Etzioni, A. (1992). Foreword in M. Zey (ed.). *Decision Making*. Newbury Park, CA: Sage.

Fisher, R., and Ury, W. (1981). *Getting to Yes*. New York: Houghton Mifflin.

Friend, J.K., Power, J.M., and Yewlett, C.J. (1974). *Public Planning: The Intercorporate*

Dimension. London: Tavistock.

Frohman, A.L. (1993). "Powering Organizations: The Case for Personal Initiative." Lexington, MA: Rath & Strong, Inc.

Gagliardi, P. (1990). *Symbols and Artifacts* (preface). Berlin: Walter de Gruyter.

Galbraith, J.K. (1983). *The Anatomy of Power*. Boston: Houghton Mifflin.

Galbraith, J.R. (1973). *Designing Complex Organizations*. Reading, MA: Addison-Wesley.

Galbraith, J.R., and Kazanjian, R.K. (1986). *Strategy Implementation*, 2nd ed. St. Paul, MN: West.

Galbraith, J.R., and Lawler, E.E., III (1993). "Challenges to the Established Order," in J.R. Galbraith, E.E. Lawler, III, and Associates, *Organizing for the Future*. San Francisco: Jossey-Bass.

Gerson, K. (1993). *No Man's Land*. New York: Basic Books.

Gharajedaghi, J. (1985). *Toward a Systems Theory of Organization*. Seaside, CA: Inter-systems Publications.

Goldhar, J.D., and Jelinek, M. (1983). "Plan for Economies of *Scope*." *Harvard Business Review*, November-December 1983, 141-48.

Greiner, L.E. (1972). "Evolution and Revolution as Organizations Grow." *Harvard Business Review*, July-August 1972, 37-46.

Grove, A.S. (1983). *High Output Management*. New York: Random House.

Grove, A.S. (1993). "PCs Trudge Out of the Valley of Death." *The Wall Street Journal*, January 18, 1993, A10.

Hale, J. (1994). *The Old Way of Seeing*. Boston: Houghton Mifflin.

Hall, E.T. (1959). *The Silent Language*. Garden City, NY: Doubleday.

Hambrick, D. (1993). "When Groups Consist of Multiple Nationalities: Toward a New Understanding of the Implications," Presenation at Academy of Management Annual Meeting, Atlanta, August 9, 1993.

Haspeslagh, P.C., and Jemison, D.B. (1991). *Managing Acquisitions*. New York: Free Press.

Henderson, B.D. (1979). *Henderson on Corporate Strategy*. New York: New American Library.

Herbst, P.G. (1976). *Alternatives to Hierarchies*. Leiden, Holland: Martinus Nijhoff.

Hersey, P., and Blanchard, K. (1982). *Management of Organizational Behavior*, 4th ed. Englewood Cliffs, NJ: Prentice-Hall.

Hirschhorn, L. (1989). "Professionals, Authority, and Group Life: A Case Study of a Law Firm," *Human Resource Management, 28* (2), 235-52.

Hirschhorn, L. (1991). *Managing in the New Team Environment*. Reading, MA: Addison-Wesley.

Hirschman, A.O. (1970). *Exit, Voice, and Loyalty*. Cambridge, MA: Harvard University.

Hofstede, G. (1991). *Culture and Organizations*. London: McGraw-Hill.

Holland, J.H. (1992). In M.M. Waldrop, *Complexity*. New York: Simon & Schuster, 185.

Hrebiniak, L.G., and Joyce, W.F. (1984). *Implementing Strategy*. New York: Macmillan.

Hronec, S.M. (1993). *Vital Signs*. New York: Amacom.

Huseman, R.C., and Alexander, E.R., III. (1979). "Communication and the Managerial Function: A Contingency Approach." In R.C. Huseman and A.B. Carroll (eds.), *Readings in Organizational Behavior*. Boston: Allyn & Bacon, 326-35.

Jackendoff, R. (1987). *Consciousness and The Computational Mind*. Cambridge, MA: MIT Press.

Jackendoff, R. (1994). *Patterns in the Mind*. New York: Basic Books.

Janis, I. (1989). *Crucial Decisions*. New York: Free Press.

Jaques, E. (1989). *Requisite Organization*. Arlington, VA: Cason Hall.

Jonas, H.S., III, Fry, R.E., and Srivastva, S. (1990). "The Office of the CEO: Understanding the Executive Experience." *Academy of Management Executive*, August 1990, 36-48.

Jones, J.C. (1967). "Trying to Design the Future," *Design*, September 1967, 35-36.

Jones, J.C. (1992). *Design Methods*, 2nd ed. New York: Van Nostrand Reinhold.

Joskowicz, L., Williams, B., Cagan, J., and Dean, T. (1993). "Design from Physical Principles." AAAI 1992 Fall Symposium Series Reports, *AI Magazine*, Spring 1993, 11.

Kahn, W.A., and Kram, K.E. (1994). "Authority at Work: Internal Models and Their Organizational Consequences," *Academy of Management Review, 19* (1), 17-50.

Kanter, R.M., Stein, B.A., and Jick, T.D. (1992). *The Challenge of Organizational Life*. New York: Free Press.

Kaplan, R.S., and Norton, D.P. (1992). "The Balanced Scoreboard—Measures that Drive Performance." *Harvard Business Review*, January-February 1992, 71-79.

Kappraff, J. (1991). *Connections*. New York: McGraw-Hill.

Katz, R.L. (1974). "Skills of an Effective Administrator," *Harvard Business Review*, September-October 1974, 90-102.

Katzenbach, J.R., and Smith, D.K. (1993). *The Wisdom of Teams*. Boston: Harvard Business School Press.

Keeley, M. (1980). "Organizational Analogy: A Comparison of Organismic and Social Contract Models." *Administrative Science Quarterly*, *25* (2), 337-62.

Keen, P.G.W. (1991). *Shaping the Future*. Boston, MA: Harvard Business School Press.

Keidel, R.W. (1982). "QWL Development: Three Trajectories." *Human Relations*, *35* (9), 743-61.

Keidel, R.W. (1984). "Baseball, Football, and Basketball: Models for Business," *Organizational Dynamics*, Winter 1984, 4-18.

Keidel, R.W. (1985). *Game Plans*. New York: Dutton.

Keidel, R.W. (1987). "Team Sports Models as a Generic Organizational Framework." *Human Relations*, *40* (9), 591-12.

Keidel, R.W. (1991). "Executive Rewards and their Impact on Teamwork." In Fred K. Foulkes (ed.), *Executive Compensation: A Strategic Guide for the 1990s*. Boston: Harvard Business School Press, 152-63.

Kelly, K. (1994). *Out of Control*. Reading, MA: Addison-Wesley.

Kiechel, W., III. (1994). "A Manager's Career in the New Economy," *Fortune*, April 4, 1994, 68-72.

Kilmann, R.H. (1989). *Managing Beyond the Quick Fix*. San Francisco: Jossey-Bass.

Kohn. A. (1993). "For Best Results, Forget the Bonus," *The New York Times*, October 17, 1993, F11.

Kosslyn, S.M., and Koenig, O. (1992). *Wet Mind*. New York: Free Press.

Kotter, J.P. (1985). *Power and Influence*. New York: Free Press.

Kotter, J.P., and Heskett, J.L. (1992). *Corporate Culture and Performance*. New York: Free Press.

Lawler, E.E., III. (1988). "Observations & Predictions of Change Processes." *Managerial Consultation Division Newsletter*, Academy of Management, *16* (2), 2-3.

Lawrence, P.R., and Dyer, D. (1983). *Renewing American Industry*. New York: Free Press.

Leavitt, H.J. (1986). *Corporate Pathfinders*. Homewood, IL: Dow Jones-Irwin.

Leo, V. (1993). Cited in F. Kofman and P.M. Senge, "Communities of Commitment: the Heart of Learning Organizations", *Organizational Dynamics*, Autumn 1993, 5-23.

Levitt, T. (1991). *Thinking About Management*. New York: Free Press.

Lewin, K. (1947). "Frontiers in Group Dynamics." In K. Lewin, *Field Theory in Social Science*, edited by D. Cartwright. Westport, CT: Greenwood Press, 1951.

Lewin, R. (1992). *Complexity*. New York: Macmillan.

Liu, Z-Y. (1993). "Qualitative Reasoning about Physical Systems with Multiple Perspectives." *AI Magazine*, Spring 1993, 77-79.

MacLean, P.D. (1978). "A Mind of Three Minds: Educating the Triune Brain." In *The 77th Yearbook of the National Society for the Study of Education*. Chicago: University of Chicago Press, 308-42.

Maidique, M.A., and Zirger, B.J. (1988). "The New Product Learning Cycle." in K. Gronhaud and G. Kaufmann (eds.), *Innovation: A Cross-Disciplinary Perspective*. Universitetsforlaget, Norway:Norwegian University Press (distributed by Oxford University Press), 407-31.

Maister, D.H. (1993). *Managing the Professional Service Firm*. New York: Free Press.

Maruyama, M. (1992). *Context and Complexity*. New York: Springer-Verlag.

Maslow, A.H. (1943). "A Theory of Human Motivation." *Psychological Review*, July 1943, 370-96.

Mayer, R.E. (1992). *Thinking, Problem Solving, Cognition*, 2nd ed. New York: W.H. Freeman.

McClelland, D.C. (1962). "Business Drive and National Achievement." *Harvard Business Review*, July-August 1962, 99-112.

McDermott, R.F. (1991). In T. Teal, "Service Comes First: An Interview with USAA's Robert F. McDermott," *Harvard Business Review*, September-October 1991, 116-27.

McGuire, M. (1991). *An Eye for Fractals*. Redwood City, CA: Addison-Wesley.

McKinsey Global Institute. (1992). *Service Sector Productivity*. Washington, DC, October 1992.

McWhinney, W. (1992). *Paths of Change*. Newbury Park, CA: Sage.

Miller, D. (1990). *The Icarus Paradox*. New York: HarperBusiness.

Miller, D., and Friesen, P.H. (1984). *Organizations: A Quantum View*. Englewood Cliffs, NJ: Prentice-Hall.

Miller, E.J. (1959). "Technology, Territory, and Time," *Human Relations, 12*, 243-72.

Minsky, M. (1985). *The Society of Mind*. New York: Simon & Schuster/Touchstone.

Mintzberg, H. (1973). "Strategy Making in Three Modes." *California Management Review*, Winter 1973, 44-53.

Mintzberg, H. (1979). *The Structuring of Organizations*. Englewood Cliffs, NJ: Prentice-Hall.

Mintzberg, H. (1989). *Mintzberg on Management*. New York: Free Press.

Mintzberg, H., and McHugh, A. (1985). "Strategy Formation in an Adhocracy." *Administrative Science Quarterly, 30* (2), 160-97.

Mitchell, C.T. (1993). *Redefining Designing*. New York: Van Nostrand Reinhold.

Mitroff, I.I., and Linstone, H.A. (1993). *The Unbounded Mind*. New York: Oxford University Press.

Modis, T. (1992). *Predictions*. New York: Simon & Schuster.

Nadler, D., and Tushman, M. (1988). *Strategic Organization Design*. Glenview, IL: Scott, Foresman.

Nute, K. (1993). *Frank Lloyd Wright and Japan*. New York: Van Nostrand Reinhold.

Nye, J.S., Jr. (1990). *Bound To Lead*. New York: Basic Books.

Oshry, B. (1986). *The Possibilities of Organization*. Boston: Power & Systems, Inc.

Ouchi, W.G. (1979). "A Conceptual Framework for the Design of Organizational Control Mechanisms." *Management Science, 25* (9), 833-48.

Ouchi, W.G. (1980). "Markets, Bureaucracies, and Clans." *Administrative Science Quarterly, 25* (1), 129-41.

Ouchi, W.G. (1981). *Theory Z*. Reading, MA: Addison-Wesley.

Ouchi, W.G. (1984). *The M-Form Society*. Reading, MA: Addison-Wesley.

Pascale, R.T., and Athos, A.G. (1981). *The Art of Japanese Management*. New York: Simon & Schuster.

Perlmutter, H.V. (1965). *Towards a Theory and Practice of Social Architecture*. London: Tavistock, Pamphlet No. 12.

Perlmutter, H.V. (1984). "Building the Symbiotic Societal Enterprise: A Social Architecture for the Future." *World Futures, 19*, 271-84.

Peters, T.J., and Waterman, R.H., Jr. (1982). *In Search of Excellence*. New York: Harper & Row.

Pfeffer, J. (1994). *Competitive Advantage through People*. Boston: Harvard Business School Press.

Piaget, J. (1974). *To Understand Is To Invent*. New York: Viking.

Pine, J. (1992). *Mass Customization*. Boston: Harvard Business School Press.

Pirsig, R.M. (1974). *Zen and the Art of Motorcycle Maintenance*. New York: Morrow.

Pondy, L.R., and Mitroff, I.I. (1979). "Beyond Open Systems Models of Organization." In B.M. Staw (ed.), *Research in Organizational Behavior*. Greenwood, CT: JAI Press, 3-39.

Porter, E.H. (1973). *Strength Deployment Inventory*. Pacific Palisades, CA: Personal Strengths Publishing.

Porter, M.E. (1980). *Competitive Strategy*. New York: Free Press.

Porter, M.E. (1985). *Competitive Advantage*. New York: Free Press.

Prokop, M.K. (1992). *Managing To Be Green*. San Diego: Pfeiffer.

Raelin, J.A. (1985). *The Clash of Cultures*. Boston: Harvard Business School Press.

Rand, P. (1993). *Design, Form, and Chaos*. New Haven, CT: Yale University Press.

Rhodes, J. (1991). *Conceptual Toolmaking*. Cambridge, MA: Basil Blackwell.

Roe, M.J. (1994) *Strong Managers, Weak Owners*. Princeton, NJ: Princeton University Press

Savage, G.T., Blair, J.D., and Sorenson, R.L. (1989). "Consider Both Relationships and Substance When Negotiating Strategically." *Academy of Management Executive*, February 1989, 37-48.

Schein, E.H. (1985). *Organizational Culture and Leadership*. San Francisco: Jossey-Bass.

Schein, E.H. (1993). "How Can Organizations Learn Faster? The Challenge of Entering the Green Room." *Sloan Management Review*, Winter 1993, 85-92.

Scholtes, P.R. (1988). *The Team Handbook*. Madison, WI: Joiner Associates.

Schrage, M. (1990). *Shared Minds*. New York: Random House.

Schutz, W. (1987). *Element B Behavior: A FIRO Instrument*. Mill Valley, CA: WSA.

Schwartz, P. (1991). *The Art of the Long View*. New York: Doubleday Currency.

Schwartz, P., and Ogilvy, J. (1979). *The Emergent Paradigm*. Menlo Park, CA: SRI International.

Scott, W.R. (1981). *Organizations*. Englewood Cliffs, NJ: Prentice-Hall.

Segal, M. (1974). "Organization and Environment: A Typology of Adaptability and Structure." *Public Administration Review*, *34*, 212-20.

Seligman, M.E.P. (1990). *Learned Optimism*. New York: Pocket Books.

Shaw, M.E. (1984). *Communication Skills and Styles*. Westport, CT: Educational Systems and Designs.

Shaw, R.B., and Perkins, D.N.T. (1992). "Teaching Organizations To Learn: The Power of Productive Failures." In D.A. Nadler, M.S. Gerstein, R.B. Shaw, and Associates, *Organizational Architecture*. San Francisco: Jossey-Bass, 175-94.

Sheridan, J.E. (1992). "Organizational Culture and Employee Retention," *Academy of Management Journal*, *35* (5), 1036-56.

Smith, C.S. (1982). *A Search for Structure*. Cambridge, MA: MIT Press.

Smith, W.E., Lethem, F.J., and Thoolen, B.A. (1980). *The Design of Organizations for Rural Development Projects—A Progress Report*. Washington, DC: World Bank Staff Working Paper No. 375, March 1980.

Spencer, B.A. (1994). "Models of Organization and Total Quality Management: A Comparison and Critical Evaluation." *Academy of Management Review*, *19* (3), 446-71.

Stata, R. (1989). "Organizational Learning—The Key to Management Innovation." *Sloan Management Review*, Spring 1989, 63-74.

Sternberg, R.E. (1988). *The Triarchic Mind*. New York: Viking.

Sundstrom, E. (1986). *Work Places*. New York: Cambridge University Press.

Tesler, L.G. (1991). "Networked Computing in the 1990s." *Scientific American*, September 1991, 86-93.

Thomas, R.J. (1992). "Organizational Change and Decision Making About New Technology." In T.A. Kochan and M. Useem (eds.), *Transforming Organizations*. New York: Oxford University Press, 280-98.

Thompson, J.D. (1967). *Organizations in Action*. New York: McGraw-Hill.

Thorngate, W. (1976). "'In General' vs. 'It Depends:' Some Comments on the Gergen-Schlenker Debate," *Personality and Social Psychology Bulletin, 2*, 404-10.

Toffler, A., and Toffler, H. (1993). "Societies at Hyper-Speed," *The New York Times*, October 31, 1993, E17.

Tomasko, R.M. (1993). *Rethinking the Corporation*. New York: Amacom.

Torrance, E.P. (1979). *The Search for Satori & Creativity*. Buffalo, NY: Creative Education Foundation.

Trist, E.L. (1976). "Action Research and Adaptive Planning." In A.W. Clark (ed.), *Experimenting with Organizational Life*. London: Plenum, 223-36.

Trist, E.L. (1983). Afterword, C. Pava, *Managing New Office Technology*. New York: Free Press, 163-75.

Trist, E.L., and Murray, H. (eds.) (1990). *The Social Engagement of Social Science, Volume I*. Philadelphia: University of Pennsylvania Press.

Trist. E.L., and Murray, H., with Trist, B. (eds.) (1993). *The Social Engagement of Social Science, Volume II*. Philadelphia: University of Pennsylvania Press.

Trist, E.L., and Murray, H., with Trist, B. (eds.) (forthcoming). *The Social Engagement of Social Science, Volume III*. Philadelphia: University of Pennsylvania Press.

Tuchman, B.W. (1980). "Mankind's Better Moments." *Wilson Quarterly*, Autumn 1980, 96-105.

Tzu, S. (1988). *The Art of War* (T. Cleary, Trans.). Boston: Shambhala.

Vroom, V.H., and Jago, A.G. (1988). *The New Leadership*. Englewood Cliffs, NJ: Prentice-Hall.

Waldrop, M. (1992). *Complexity*. New York: Simon & Schuster.

Wallen, R.W. (1963). "The 3 Types of Executive Personality." *Dun's Review and Modern Industry*, February 1963, 54-56, 106.

Walton, R.E. (1989). *Up and Running*. Boston, MA: Harvard Business School Press.

Warnecke, H.J. (1993). *The Fractal Company*. Berlin: Springer-Verlag.

Weick, K.E., and Roberts, K.H. (1993). "Collective Mind in Organizations: Heedful Interrelating on Flight Decks," *Administrative Science Quarterly, 38* (3), 357-81.

Weisbord, M.R. (1992). *Discovering Common Ground*. San Francisco: Berrett-Koehler.

Welch, J.F., Jr. (1993). In N.M. Tichy and S. Sherman, *Control Your Destiny or Someone Else Will*. New York: Doubleday Currency.

Wheatley, M.J. (1992). *Leadership and The New Science*. San Francisco: Berrett-Koehler.

Wheelwright, S.C., and Clark, K.B. (1992). *Revolutionizing Product Development*. New York: Free Press.

Wills, G. (1994). *Certain Trumpets*. New York: Simon & Schuster.

Womack, J.P., and Jones, D.T. (1994). "From Lean Production to the Lean Enterprise," *Harvard Business Review*, March-April 1994, 93-103.

Womack, J.P., Jones, D.T., and Roos, D. (1990). *The Machine that Changed the World*. New York: Macmillan.

Woodward, J. (1965). *Industrial Organization*. London: Oxford University Press.

Wright, F.L. (1945). *An Autobiography*. London: Faber & Faber, and Hyperion Press.

Yearout, S., and Hammond, J. (1992). "Competitiveness: Where America Really Stands in the World." *Boardroom Reports*, February 15, 1992, 10.

NOTES

Preface

1. John Seely Brown, quoted by Rick Tetzeli in "Surviving Information Overload," *Fortune*, July 11, 1994, 65.

2. Frank Oppenheimer, quoted by Margaret J. Wheatley in *Leadership and the New Science* (San Francisco: Berrett-Koehler, 1992), 13.

Chapter 1. The Triadic Nature of Organization

1. This example originally appeared in Robert W. Keidel, "Baseball, Football, and Basketball: Models for Business," *Organizational Dynamics*, Winter 1984, 7.

2. These three patterns can also be viewed developmentally. Thus, it is possible to characterize contrasting states of race relations in the U.S. South (and indeed, throughout the nation): (1) slavery (control), (2) so-called "separate but equal" status (autonomy—at least in name; more accurately, de facto control), and (3) true integration (cooperation). Although opinions differ widely about the current mix, few would claim that American society is yet deeply integrated across racial lines.

3. In particular, I was attempting to describe and explain the structural essence of James D. Thompson's *Organizations in Action* (New York: McGraw-Hill, 1967)—viz., Thompson's three forms of *task interdependence* (as I discuss in chapter 5 of this book) and such related triadic concepts of his as *coordination, technologies, factors influencing organizational rationality,* and *cooperative strategies for acquiring power.*

4. A notable exception is the work of Henry Mintzberg, who has elegantly graphed the shapes of different structural configurations. See, in particular, *The Structuring of Organizations* (Englewood Cliffs, NJ: Prentice-Hall, 1979).

5. N.E. Thing Enterprises, *Magic Eye* (Kansas City: Andrews and McMeel, 1993). Thanks to Joel DeLuca for bringing this work—and its metaphorical implications—to my attention. One of several subsequent books on "stereograms," Dan Dyckman's *Hidden Dimensions* (New York: Harmony Books, 1994), is perhaps an even better metaphor for *Seeing Organizational Patterns* because it presents *systems* of graphics (in the form of mazes, puzzles, and mirror images)—much like the related sets of triangles that I describe.

6. R. Buckminster Fuller, *Synergetics* (New York: Macmillan/Collier Books, 1982), 319.

7. Margaret J. Wheatley, *Leadership and the New Science* (San Francisco: Berrett-Koehler, 1992), 143.

8. This and the following two-way contrasts are taken from Robert W. Keidel, "Triangular Design: A New Organizational Geometry," *Academy of Management*

Executive, November 1990, 25.

9. Tracy Kidder, *The Soul of a New Machine* (New York: Avon Books, 1981), 120.

10. *Ibid.*, 288.

11. Christopher Alexander, in *The Timeless Way of Building* (New York: Oxford, 1979), 147–48, argues that "There is an indefinable roughness, a looseness, a relaxedness, which nature always has . . . . " Conceptually similar to this pattern are the insights of a branch of applied mathematics called "fuzzy logic." See, for example, Bart Kosko, *Fuzzy Thinking* (New York: Hyperion, 1993).

Chapter 2. Varieties of Design Failure

1. Support for this position is provided by K. Anders Ericsson and Neil Charness in "Expert Performance: Its Structure and Acquisition," *American Psychologist*, August 1994, 745: "There is no reason to believe that changes in the structure of human performance and skill are restricted to the traditional domains of expertise. Similar changes should be expected in many everyday activities, such as thinking, comprehension, and problem solving, studied in general psychology." Minimally, Jay Conger's observations about realistic expectations concerning leadership programs (Jay A. Conger, *Learning to Lead* [San Francisco: Jossey-Bass, 1992], 181) apply to learning about thinking: "Realistically . . . , we might expect that a well-designed leadership program could result in something roughly like the following: (1) no behavioral change and little enhanced awareness for perhaps 10 to 20 percent of participants, (2) an expanded conceptual understanding of leadership for another 30 to 40 percent, (3) some positive though incremental behavioral change (in addition to a conceptual understanding) for an additional 25 to 30 percent, and (4) significant positive behavioral change for 10 percent. If a program can enhance the leadership abilities of just these percentages alone, I believe it is worth the time and expenditure. I also believe, however, that the potential could be higher with better preselection of participants and more powerful educational experiences."

2. In fact, there is a fourth way to fail: having the *wrong* priorities—so that a mismatch exists between organizational design and strategic direction.

3. Ray Stata, "Organizational Learning—The Key to Management Innovation," *Sloan Management Review*, Spring 1989, 67.

4. "America's Vigilante Values," *The Economist*, June 20, 1990, 17–18.

5. Richard Reeves, "In Los Angeles, Diversity in the Schools Is Being Taken To Its Logical End—Chaos," *The Philadelphia Inquirer*, December 28, 1992, A12.

6. Eduard A. Shevardnadze, quoted in "Shevardnadze: Nuclear Menace Is Real," *The Philadelphia Inquirer*, December 31, 1991, A4.

7. "Growing Pains at People Express," *Business Week*, January 28, 1985, 91.

8. Often the line is difficult to draw between too little control at a higher system level and too much autonomy at a lower system level. Many situations can be characterized either way—or both ways.

9. For a thoughtful discussion of organizational boundaries, see Larry Hirschhorn and Thomas Gilmore, "The New Boundaries of the 'Boundaryless' Company," *Harvard Business Review*, May–June 1992, 104–15.

10. Michael Schrage, *Shared Minds* (New York: Random House, 1990), 44.

11. Jeffrey Pfeffer, *Competitive Advantage Through People* (Boston: Harvard Business School Press, 1994), 111.

12. At the same time, many 2x2 matrices reduce to triangles since one cell (typically that which signifies low/low, no/no, or negative/negative) represents either a nonoption or a nonviable option. An example that parallels autonomy/control/cooperation is the grid featured in Philippe C. Haspeslagh and David B. Jemison's *Managing Acquisitions* (New York: Free Press, 1991), 145. Its dimensions are (1) need for organizational autonomy [low/high] and (2) need for strategic interdependence (low/high). There are three legitimate strategies: *preservation* (autonomy), *absorption* (control), and *symbiosis* (cooperation). A "holding" strategy (which is low/low) is essentially a nonstrategy. Haspeslagh and Jemison (146–47) characterize such a tack as an acquisition in which "the firm has no intention of integrating and creating value through anything except financial transfers, risk-sharing, or general management capability, even though the two firms are presumably in such similar businesses that there is no need for organizational autonomy. The only integration in such acquisitions would, in a sense, be a mere holding activity."

13. Indeed, even when a two-variable process appears to succeed, by producing a "win-win," a third perspective—often representing contextual or community interests—may suffer; a classic example of this pattern is collusion, at the public's expense. A note on philosophy. John W. Chandler has helped me to see that triangular thinking bridges Hegelian inquiring systems (in which each synthesis becomes the thesis in a subsequent triad) and Kantian inquiring systems (in which the consideration of multiple perspectives gives birth to a creative blend). A useful summary of these and other methods of inquiry is Marjorie A. Lyles and Ian I. Mitroff, "Organizational Problem Formulation: An Empirical Study," *Administrative Science Quarterly*, 25 (1), March 1980, 102-19.

14. An important qualification is in order. Although triangular thinking is widely appropriate to organizational issues, one- and two-variable patterns each have their situational relevance. (See Robert W. Keidel, "Cognitive Patterns: A Variables-Based Interpretation," presentation, 52nd Annual Meeting, Academy of Management, Atlanta, August 10, 1993. This essay describes thinking patterns in terms of both the number of variables that they address and the *geometries* that they represent, including *point* [one-variable], *linear* [two-variable compromise], and *angular* [two variable combination], as well as *triangular*.)

Philosophical support for *triangular* thinking (and design/management) comes from Ian I. Mitroff and Harold A. Linstone, *The Unbounded Mind* (New York: Oxford, 1993). Mitroff and Linstone advocate *unbounded systems thinking*, which blends three perspectives: *personal/individual* (autonomy), *technical* (control), and *organizational/societal* (cooperation).

Additional theoretical support is provided indirectly by Japanese organization theorist Magoroh Maruyama, "Changing Dimensions in International Business," *Academy of Management Executive*, August 1992, 88–96. Maruyama defines four types of *mindscape*—a term that denotes (92) "the way a person organizes his/her thinking and behavior." He asserts (92) that these "types and their mixtures account for about two-thirds of people in most cultures." Maruyama's mindscape types are as follows:

I-type	H-type	S-type	G-type
heterogenist	homogenist	heterogenist	heterogenist
isolationist	hierarchical	interactive	interactive
temporary	permanent	stability	change
laissez-faire	competitive	cooperative	cogenerative
randomizing	classifying	contextual	contextual
haphazard	sequential	simultaneous	simultaneous
subjective	one truth	many truths	many truths
negative-sum	zero-sum	positive-sum	positive-sum

The similarities between S-type and G-type appear to be more compelling than the differences; consequently, the four types appear to cluster into a triad—I/H/SG—that roughly corresponds to autonomy/control/cooperation.

Finally, Joanne Martin in *Cultures in Organizations* (New York: Oxford, 1992) describes three cultural perspectives, each of which parallels a different but symmetrical two-variable blend: *differentiation* (autonomy/control), *integration* (control/cooperation), and *fragmentation* (autonomy/cooperation).

15. David A. Nadler and Michael L. Tushman, in "Organizational Frame Bending: Principles for Managing Reorientation," *Academy of Management Executive*, August 1989, 199, posit the *three-theme principle*: "As a general rule, managers of a change can only initiate and sustain approximately three key themes during any particular period of time."

16. Peter Schwartz, *The Art of the Long View* (New York: Doubleday Currency, 1991), 146. Schwartz's perspective is shared by Alan D. Meyer, Anne S. Tsui, and C.R. Hinings in "Configurational Approaches to Organizational Analysis," *Academy Management Journal, 36* (6), December 1993, 1181–82: "Critics have charged that some classification schemes oversimplify reality and fail to reflect the complexity of organizational life . . . . In particular, classifications based upon only one or two dimensions have been criticized . . . . We too believe that organizational configurations incorporating multiple dimensions are apt to prove most valuable in both theoretical and empirical applications. But there is a trade-off. As dimensions are added to increase congruence with reality, configurations necessarily grow more complex and unwieldy. It would be naive to think that the perfect taxonomy is the one that perfectly replicates reality. Even if such a taxonomy could be constructed, its specificity would defeat its purpose—to generalize and abstract."

17. D.M. Considine (ed.), *Van Nostrand's Scientific Encyclopedia* (New York: Van

Nostrand Reinhold, 1976), 615.

Chapter 3. Triangulating Autonomy, Control, and Cooperation

1. In exhibit 1-2, I linked business process *reengineering* not with cooperation, but with control (and, secondarily, with autonomy). In terms of reengineering, exhibit 1-2 describes my impression of what typically *is;* exhibit 3-1 depicts what *should be.*

2. The following account is taken from Robert W. Keidel, "Triangular Design: A New Organizational Geometry," *Academy of Management Executive,* November 1990, 29–32; exhibit 3-2 is an updated version of the graphic that appeared in that paper.

3. Paul R. Lawrence and Jay W. Lorsch, *Organization and Environment* (Boston: Harvard University, 1967), 11.

4. George F. Mechlin and Daniel Berg, "Evaluating Research—ROI Is Not Enough," *Harvard Business Review,* September-October 1980, 94.

5. The concept of marketing as "middleman" is discussed in Derek F. Abell, *Managing with Dual Strategies* (New York: Free Press, 1993), 242–43.

6. Many training departments are routinely approached by individuals with non-training needs. An "individual problems" triangle that I developed has helped some training/development managers to screen out inappropriate candidates. The corners of this graphic are *capacity* (autonomy), *skill* (control), and *motivation* (cooperation). In general, training is most useful for skill-building. Issues of capacity have to do chiefly with selection/placement, while motivational problems may have a wide range of causes.

7. Terry Winograd and Fernando Flores, *Understanding Computers and Cognition* (Reading, MA: Addison-Wesley, 1986), 143–62.

8. Alan Webber, "What's So New About the New Economy?" *Harvard Business Review,* January-February 1993, 30.

9. This instrument has been refined continuously since 1982. The profile has ranged in length from six dimensions to twenty-five, and has been used in one or another form with hundreds of groups—primarily in corporations but also in professional service firms, universities, governmental agencies, non-profit organizations, branches of the military, and professional sports teams. Similarly, the Organizational Design Triangle has evolved with use. Some of the exhibits in this book were actually cast in terms of an earlier graphic (that was not able to capture the absence of one variable).

10. See Robert W. Keidel, *A Concept of Organizational Design,* Occasional Paper #1, Organization & Management Series, Washington, DC: The World Bank, May 1993. The author, in *Corporate Players* (New York: Wiley, 1988), 207–12, arrays ten representative checklists in terms of various combinations of organizational strategy, structure, and style.

11. Jeffrey Pfeffer, *Competitive Advantage Through People* (Boston: Harvard Business School Press, 1994), 64.

12. Jonathan Hale, *The Old Way of Seeing* (Boston: Houghton Mifflin, 1994), 68.

13. One of the most striking examples of such anomaly—and the danger of characterizing an organization based on its chart alone—is reported in Homa Bahrami and Stuart Evans, "Stratocracy in High-Technology Firms," *California Management Review*, Fall 1987, 51–66. The authors describe a $500 million telecommunications company that, although functionally structured on paper (a *control* pattern, as discussed in chapter 5), is distinguished by a wide array of *cooperative* processes—including shared objectives, extensive consultation and communication, managerial rotation, abundant task forces and project teams, and an integrative system of meetings.

Nitin Nohria and James D. Berkley (in "An Action Perspective: The Crux of the New Management," *California Management Review*, Summer 1994, 70–92) note a similar pattern with respect to the Industrial Computer and Control Group (ICCG) of Allen-Bradley, a Rockwell International subsidiary. Although a novel, "concentric" design was replaced with a more traditional, hierarchical structure, cooperative, teamwork-oriented behavior across divisions and functions persisted. Nohria and Berkley conclude (78) that "ICCG realizes that the group's formal organization as it exists on paper is not what matters."

Chapter 4. Organizational Strategy

1. Susan Antilla, "'Most Admired'—by Short Sellers, Too," *The New York Times*, February 14, 1993, F13.

2. Michael Schrage, "Fire Your Customers!" *The Wall Street Journal*, March 16, 1992, A14.

3. Charles Hampden-Turner, *Charting the Corporate Mind* (New York: Free Press, 1990), 6.

4. My concept of *organizational character* is equivalent to *institutional strategy* as articulated by Richard G. Hamermesh in *Making Strategy Work* (New York: Wiley, 1986), 36: "the basic character and vision of the company." By contrast, *corporate strategy* refers to "the determination of the businesses in which a company will compete and the allocation of resources among the businesses" (36); and *business strategy* is "the competitive strategy of a particular business unit" (34).

5. This account is taken from Bernard Wysocki, Jr., "The Chief's Personality Can Have a Big Impact—For Better or Worse," *The Wall Street Journal*, September 11, 1984, 1, 12.

6. Wally Olins, *Corporate Identity* (Boston: Harvard Business School Press, 1989).

7. Paul Hawken, *The Ecology of Commerce* (New York: HarperBusiness, 1993).

8. Howell Raines, quoted by Ken Auletta in "Opening Up The Times," *The New Yorker*, July 28, 1993, 65.

9. E.S. Browning, "Long-Term Thinking and Paternalistic Ways Carry Michelin To Top," *The Wall Street Journal*, January 5, 1990, A1. According to a more recent account (E.S. Browning, "Michelin Is Setting Out on the Road to Transformation," *The Wall Street Journal*, September 24, 1994, B4), Michelin is trying to become less secretive.

10. Stratford Sherman, "Are Strategic Alliances Working?" *Fortune*, September 21, 1992, 77–78.

11. David H. Maister in *Managing the Professional Service Firm* (New York: Free Press, 1993) presents a variation on this triad for professional service firms in general: *brains* work (expertise), *procedure* work (efficiency), and *gray hair* work (experience). Weld Coxe, Nina F. Hartung, Hugh H. Hochberg, Brian J. Lewis, David H. Maister, Robert F. Mattox, and Peter A. Piven in "Charting Your Course" (*Architectural Technology*, May/June 1986, 52–58), adapt Maister's framework to architecture firms, which they categorize as competing on the basis of *strong idea* or *strong delivery* or *strong service*.

12. Two of the three performance priorities—*differentiation* and *cost* (leadership)—match generic competitive strategies previously articulated by Michael Porter in *Competitive Strategy* (New York: Free Press, 1980); and *Competitive Advantage* (New York: Free Press, 1985). The third performance priority that I identify—*flexibility*—overlaps Porter's "focus" strategy.

13. A fourth component is *opportunity cost*—the value forgone by investing in a particular product/service instead of some other(s). Opportunity cost may be regarded as a context within which the other three costs are incurred.

14. Paul Rand, *Design, Form, and Chaos* (New Haven, CT: Yale University Press, 1993), 19.

15. Joel Birnbaum, quoted by Laurence Hooper in "Who's a Genius?" *The Wall Street Journal*, May 24, 1993, R18. Birnbaum's assertion is backed up by Thomas A. Bass, *Reinventing the Future* (Reading, MA: Addison-Wesley, 1994)—a study of eleven prominent scientists that demonstrates the link between creativity and independence.

16. Thomas E. Everhart, quoted by John Carey, et al., in "Could America Afford the Transistor Today?" *Business Week*, March 1994, 84.

17. Actually there are *twenty-six* ways to prioritize differentiation, cost, and flexibility, as an organization may have no priorities whatsoever—and therefore, fall outside the triangle. But such a posture is equivalent to being stuck in the middle of the triangle (CFD), that is, trying for the best of all three worlds and realizing none of these. In either case, the organization fails to exercise choice.

18. Danny Miller, *The Icarus Paradox* (New York: HarperBusiness, 1990), 33.

19. Thomas S. Monaghan, quoted by Krystal Miller and Richard Gibson in "Dominos Stops Promising Pizza in 30 Minutes," *The Wall Street Journal*, December 22, 1993, B1.

20. James L. Heskett, W. Earl Sasser, Jr., and Christopher W.L. Hart, *Service Breakthroughs* (New York: Free Press, 1990).

Chapter 5. Organiztional Structure

1. "Keep Ahead of Your Competition with The Organization Chart Collection, 1992–1993" (New York: The Conference Board, 1993).

2. This example is taken from Jessica Lipnack and Jeffrey Stamps, *The TeamNet Factor* (Essex Junction, VT: Oliver Wight, 1993), 63–64.

3. Tracy Kidder, *The Soul of a New Machine* (New York: Avon Books, 1981), 120.

4. A complex example of a team-based chart is that for Ford Motor Co.'s *Team Taurus*, as presented in David C. Smith, "Team Taurus: Ford's $3-Billion Mid-Market Plunge," *Ward's Auto World*, February 1985, 29 (and drawn by Gloria Moriarty).

5. David H. Maister, *Managing the Professional Service Firm* (New York: Free Press, 1993), 7.

6. Richard Rosecrance, "Too Many Bosses, Too Few Workers," *The New York Times*, July 15, 1990, F11.

7. This triangle can also be used to describe alternative meeting-room and classroom formats. An *autonomy* equivalent is a space containing several freestanding tables, desks, or workstations. A *control* equivalent is an auditorium-type arrangement designed for one individual—such as a lecturer or a stand-up trainer—to speak in a one-way manner to a large, passive audience. A *cooperation* equivalent is literally a round (square) table or a horseshoe that enables and encourages everyone to interact with everyone else.

8. Alan Deutschman, "The Managing Wisdom of High-Tech Superstars," *Fortune*, October 17, 1994, 197–206.

9. Edward R. Tufte, quoted by Stuart Silverstone in "Saying It with Images: An Interview with Edward Tufte," *Aldus Magazine*, May/June 1991, 29.

10. Christopher Alexander, Sara Ishikawa, and Murray Silverstein, with Max Jacobson, Ingrid Fiksdahl-King, and Shlomo Angel, *A Pattern Language* (New York: Oxford, 1977), 410-11

11. This example is taken from Stephen Fox, *The Mirror Makers* (New York: Morrow, 1984), 252-55.

Chapter 6. Organizational Systems

1. A 1993 survey conducted by the *Chronicle of Philanthropy*, a publication that covers nonprofits, cited by Robin Goldwyn Blumenthal in "Survey Says Most Nonprofit Groups Paid Chief Executives Over $100,000 Yearly," *The Wall Street Journal*, April 5, 1993, B7D.

2. "Deflating Uncle Sam's Bureaucratic Bloat," *Business Week*, September 13, 1993, 110.

3. T.J. Rodgers, William Taylor, and Rick Foreman, *No Excuses Management* (New York: Doubleday Currency, 1993).

4. John A. Byrne, with Lori Bongiorno and Ronald Grover, "That Eye-Popping Executive Pay," *Business Week*, April 25, 1994, 52–58.

5. Ken Iverson, quoted in "Face-to-Face," *Inc.*, April 1986, 44.

6. Kevin Kelly, "A CEO Who Kept His Eyes on the Horizon," *Business Week*, August 1, 1994, 32.

7. Robert Neff, "What Do Japanese CEOs *Really* Make?" *Business Week*, April 26, 1993, 60–61.

8. Richard Behar, "The Last-Minute Money Grab," *Time*, March 5, 1990, 44.

9. Alan Deutschman, "The Managing Wisdom of High-Tech Superstars," *Fortune*, October 17, 1994, 197–206.

10. Stanley Bing, "Sure Cures for the Madness of Meetings," *The New York Times*, December 19, 1993, F13.

11. Stephen Baker (with drawings by Arnie Levin), *I Hate Meetings* (New York, Macmillan, 1983).

12. Andrew S. Grove, *High Output Management* (New York: Random House, 1983), 71.

13. The earliest use of the term *meeting system* of which I am aware is that by Lynn Oppenheim, who has explored the relationship between focal meetings and (1) patterns of preparation and follow-up, and (2) other meetings and organizational mechanisms, such as information systems and reporting relations. See Lynn Oppenheim, *Making Meetings Matter* (Philadelphia: Wharton Center for Applied Research [now known as the Center for Applied Research], 1988).

14. An abbreviated version of this section appeared in Robert W. Keidel, "Only Three Reasons to Meet," *Management Review*, May 1991, 5.

15. These activities parallel what Andrew S. Grove, *op. cit.*, 89–93, describes as the

ideal decision-making process: *free discussion, clear direction,* and *full support.* They also mirror three criteria that organizational theorist Chris Argyris, in *Intervention Theory and Method* (Reading, MA: Addison-Wesley, 1973), 16–20, specifies for change "intervention": *valid information; free, informed choice;* and *internal commitment* to the choices made.

16. Richard J. Censits, quoted by Damon Darlin in "Road Can Be Bumpy When New Chief Acts to Envliven His Firm," *The Wall Street Journal,* September 17, 1984, 10.

17. Rob Davis, quoted by George Harrar in "Baldridge Notwithstanding," *Forbes ASAP,* February 28, 1994, 46.

18 . The comments on downsizing are based on a survey by Philadelphia consultant Right Associates, cited in "Pink-slip Productivity," *The Economist,* March 28, 1992, 79.

19. The following account is taken from Jerald Greenberg in *Security,* cited in *Boardroom Reports,* May 15, 1991, 2.

20. Indeed, if one combines decision-making and implementation, then collaboration (consensus) in its own right appears to be "fast." The time lost in generating understanding and commitment is more than recovered in terms of speed of implementation. Such a pattern (which has often been used to characterize typical Japanese styles) is summed up by the well-known Fram oil filter commercial: "Pay me now, or pay me later." The meaning: Those who pay later, pay greater.

21. The discussion and quotations that follow are taken from Kathleen M. Eisenhardt, "Making Fast Strategic Decisions in High-Velocity Environments," *Academy of Management Journal, 32* (3), September 1989, 543–76. A more popular version of this paper is Kathleen M. Eisenhardt, "Speed and Strategic Choice: How Managers Accelerate Decision Making," *California Management Review,"* Spring 1990, 39–54.

22. The following discussion and quotation are taken from Herbert A. Simon, "Making Management Decisions: The Role of Intuition and Emotion," *Academy of Management Executive,* February 1987, 59–60.

23. Calvin H.P. Pava, *Managing New Office Technology* (New York: Free Press, 1983), 58. The following discussion and quotations are taken from pp. 58–60. A similar concept of *deliberation* is presented in Terry Winograd and Fernando Flores, *Understanding Computers and Cognition* (Reading, MA: Addison-Wesley, 1986), 149–50.

24. "Research and Disillusionment," *The Economist,* April 13, 1991, 63.

25. Voting is especially apt to polarize a team that congregates face-to-face. When people "meet" anonymously, as in certain electronic meetings, polarization appears to be less of a problem (or perhaps not a problem at all). But the jury is still out on the degree to which such computerized meetings can contribute to organizational effectiveness and learning—and commitment—as opposed to the efficiency of the decision-making process.

26. Ian I. Mitroff and Harold A. Linstone, *The Unbounded Mind* (New York: Oxford, 1993), 146.

27. These figures are derived from a chart titled "Teaming up," in "Science Survey," *The Economist*, February 16, 1991, 5.

28. Daniel E. Koshland, Jr., "Methodology and Theory at the Frontier," *Science*, March 27, 1992, 1621.

Chapter 7. Toward An Organizational Pattern Language

1. Kurt Lewin, "Frontiers in Group Dynamics," in Dorwin Cartwright (ed.), *Field Theory in Social Science: Selected Theoretical Papers by Kurt Lewin* (Westport, CT: Greenwood Press, 1951).

2. The issue here is largely one of *internal fit* (i.e., consistency among organizational elements) vs. *external fit* (organization:environment). Ideally, responses to internal and external demands will form a mutually-reinforcing whole. In a turbulent environment, however, such a state may be impossible to achieve. According to Richard D'Aveni (with Robert Gunther) in *Hypercompetition* (New York: Free Press, 1994), 239: "Advantage is said to be created if a firm focuses all its parts on one consistent goal and purpose that the external environment is willing to pay for. This may work well in fairly stable environments. But when the environment is one of increasing uncertainty and rapid change, the concept of internal fit becomes more problematic." D'Aveni's argument is consistent with that expressed in Danny Miller and Peter H. Friesen, *Organizations: A Quantum View* (Englewood Cliffs, NJ: Prentice-Hall, 1984), 266: "quantum and dramatic structural changes seem to be more closely associated with high performance than piecemeal and incremental structural changes."

3. Shojiro Sugiyama, *25 Shoto-kan KATA*, 2nd edition (Chicago: S. Sugiyama, 1989).

4. Christopher Alexander, Sara Ishikawa, and Murray Silverstein, with Max Jacobson, Ingrid Fiksdahl-King, and Shlomo Angel, *A Pattern Language* (New York: Oxford, 1977).

5. Christopher Alexander, *The Timeless Way of Building* (New York: Oxford, 1979), 247.

6. Alexander et al., *op. cit.*, 469, 471–72.

7. Jonathan Hale, *The Old Way of Seeing* (Boston: Houghton Mifflin, 1994), 45.

8. Apart from the work of Alexander and Hale, the greatest relevance of architecture to the concepts developed in this book appears to lie in the philosophy of Frank Lloyd Wright: "Wright's buildings . . . were intended be less like realistic *portraits* of their programmes, than idealized 'conventions,' encapsulating in simple geometric terms what he considered to be the characterizing features of a particular client or institution. . . . Wright appears to have seen his own role as one of providing geometric abstractions of the fundamental social forms of American life. Or as Robert Twombly put it: 'Behind social insti-

tutions, Wright insisted, was the artist's vision, for he alone could translate into structure and form the essence of what it meant to be human and live happily with others.' And in practice, this meant reducing those institutions to their formal essence and then re-presenting their 'essential forms' in terms of a simple geometric unit arranged into a mutually interdependent 'organic' whole" (Kevin Nute, *Frank Lloyd Wright and Japan* [New York: Van Nostrand Reinhold, 1993], 107).

9. Japanese organization theorist Magoroh Maruyama, in "Changing Dimensions in International Business" (*Academy of Management Executive*, August 1992, 88–96) has shown that Western architecture is based on principles of similarity, repetition, opposition, tension, and extension. By contrast, Japanese patterns emphasize interaction, complementarity, continuity, and convertibility—as exemplified by traditional Japanese houses, in which internal, horizontal boundaries can be reshaped to fit various functions. Maruyama observes that this contrast plays out in terms of divergent managerial/organizational philosophies.

10. A notable exception is Howard Perlmutter, who coined the term "social architecture" to refer to a values-based process of building *indispensable institutions*, as opposed to *expendable organizations* and *destructive organizations*. See Howard V. Perlmutter, *Towards a Theory and Practice of Social Architecture* (London: Tavistock Publications, 1965).

11. Alexander, *op. cit.,* 199.

12. A significant caveat is in order concerning art vis-a-vis architecture. Architects who behave as though architecture *is* art are likely to lose touch with users and their needs. C. Thomas Mitchell in *Redefining Designing* (New York: Van Nostrand Reinhold, 1993), 27–28, expresses exactly this caution with respect to certain strains of contemporary architecture: "The key aspect of late modern and deconstructive architecture seems not to be the formal properties of either, but rather their total disregard of design users. They are hermetically sealed approaches to architecture as a fine art whose practitioners believe themselves to be without any social purpose or under any obligation to the public."

13. In *On Purposeful Systems* (Chicago: Aldine-Atherton, 1972), 215, Russell L. Ackoff and Fred E. Emery argue the following about social systems: "There is a constant tendency toward *increasing* or *decreasing variety* in the range and level of the behavior of the elements. In that the individual elements are instrumental to the system, the system will be *variety decreasing*: the range of purposeful behavior will be restricted, and increasingly behavior will be at a lower level of multi-goal-seeking or goal-seeking behavior. In that the system is instrumental to its component elements, it will tend to be *variety increasing*: the range of purposeful behavior will be extended, and increasingly behavior will be at the higher level of ideal-seeking."

14. Cyril Stanley Smith, *A Search for Structure* (Cambridge, MA: MIT Press, 1982), 358.

15. Christopher Alexander, *A Foreshadowing of 21st Century Art* (New York: Oxford, 1993), 35–36.

16. The idea here is similar to P.G. Herbst's principle of "minimal critical specification"—i.e., defining only broad, essential parameters in order to maximize future adaptability. See P.G. Herbst, *Socio-Technical Design* (London: Tavistock, 1974), 19–27. A complementary approach is Gareth Morgan's provocative notion of ruling *out* noxiants (rather than ruling *in* desired parameters). See Gareth Morgan, *Images of Organization* (Beverly Hills, CA: Sage, 1986), 106–07.

The importance of acknowledging individual visions, and encouraging their interaction in order to coalesce a shared vision, is forcefully articulated by Peter Senge in *The Fifth Discipline* (New York: Doubleday Currency, 1990), 217–18: "Visions that are truly shared take time to emerge. They grow as a by-product of interactions of individual visions. Experience suggests that visions that are genuinely shared require ongoing conversation where individuals not only feel free to express their dreams, but learn how to listen to each others' dreams . . . . [W]e must allow multiple visions to coexist, listening for the right course of action that transcends and unifies all our individual visions."

17. Annemarie Schimmel, *The Mystery of Numbers* (New York: Oxford, 1993), 59.

18. *Ibid.*, 60.

19. R. Buckminster Fuller, *Synergetics* (New York: Macmillan/Collier Books, 1982), 602.

20. Peter Schwartz, *The Art of the Long View* (New York: Doubleday Currency, 1991), 147.

21. The fact of incompleteness in human experience has been captured in a negative sense by Greek mythology's Achilles' heel; and in a positive sense by Laotzu, as translated by Amos Ih Tiao Chang in *The Tao of Architecture* (Princeton, NJ: Princeton University Press, 1956), 26: "To him who regards nothing as persistent, what is essentially important in things is the possibility of becoming something, not the opportunity of remaining as something confronting deterioration. Consequently, meaningful incompletion is taken as the most desirable state of tangible being." More recently, Laotzu's perspective has been philosophically described in terms of cognition by Francisco J. Varela, Evan Thompson, and Eleanor Rosch in *The Embodied Mind* (Cambridge, MA: MIT Press, 1991), 205; poignantly conveyed as visual humor in Shel Silverstein's children's cartoon story, *The Missing Piece* (New York: Harper & Row, 1976); and expressed in song by Leonard Cohen's "Anthem" ("There is a crack in everything./That's how the light gets in."), *The Future* (Sony Music Entertainment, 1992). Abstractly, Kurt Gödel demonstrated through his incompleteness theorem that no theory of all mathematics is finitely describable, consistent, and complete (Rudy Rucker, *Mind Tools* [Boston: Houghton Mifflin, 1987], 218–26).

22. Ian I. Mitroff and Harold A. Linstone, *The Unbounded Mind* (New York: Oxford, 1993), 108–09.

23. "Stickiness" has philosophical roots in Martin Heidegger's concept of *thrownness*—the notion that we are ever thrown into situations (contexts) that necessarily affect our behavior. Terry Winograd and Fernando Flores in *Understanding Computers and*

Cognition (Reading, MA: Addison-Wesley, 1986) discuss thrownness at length. They note (35–36) that "Our interactions with other people and with the inanimate world we inhabit put us into a situation of thrownness, for which the metaphor of the meeting is much more apt than the metaphor of the objective detached scientist who makes observations, forms hypotheses, and consciously chooses a rational course of action."

24. Henry Mintzberg, *Mintzberg on Management* (New York: Free Press, 1989), 356.

25. Abraham Kaplan, *The Conduct of Inquiry* (San Francisco: Chandler, 1964), 298.

26. See, for example, M.C. Escher, *Escher on Escher* (Trans. Karin Ford) (New York: Abrams, 1986). A beautiful summary of Escher's work is Doris Schattschneider, *Visions of Symmetry* (New York: W.H. Freeman, 1990).

27. Benoit B. Mandelbrot, *The Fractal Character of Nature* (New York: W.H. Freeman, 1983), 1. Mandelbrot's work has been popularized by James Gleick in *Chaos* (New York: Viking, 1987).

28. The Sierpinski Triangle is discussed at length in Michael Field and Martin Golubitsky, *Symmetry in Chaos* (New York: Oxford, 1992).

29. See Robert W. Keidel, "Theme Appreciation as a Construct for Organizational Change," *Management Science*, 27 (11), November 1981, 1261–78.

30. Two of the five icons in exhibit 7-6 differ somewhat from those that made up the original graphic.

31. Cyril Stanley Smith, *op. cit.*, 325.

32. *Ibid.*, 328–30.

33. Fred Kofman and Peter M. Senge, "Communities of Commitment: The Heart of Learning Organizations," *Organizational Dynamics*, Autumn 1993, 22. The concept of a "practice field" fits David Garvin's argument that learning (and in my view, creative thinking) involves an overlapping three-step process: Cognitive change produces behavioral change, which then leads to performance improvement. In other words, some preliminary work must occur before positive results are realized. See David A. Garvin, "Building a Learning Organization," *Harvard Business Review*, July-August 1993, 78–91. A similar perspective with respect to physical design was articulated more than thirty years ago by architect John Christopher Jones in "A Method of Systematic Design," in J.C. Jones & D.G. Thornley (eds.), *Conference on Design Methods* (Oxford: Pergamon Press, 1963), 64: "The great difficulty of introducing Systematic Design is that its advantages are not obtained in first attempts. Successful application is much more likely when changes in organization have been introduced beforehand. As with many new things it involves an acclimatization period during which things may get worse before they get better."

34. A seemingly contradictory perspective is that some measure of dissonance or "stretch" is essential to change (Gary Hamel and C.K. Prahalad, *Competing for the Future*

[Boston: Harvard Business School Press, 1994]). The issue here is similar to those of (1) *basic* R&D (discovery/invention) vs. *applied* R&D (application/innovation)—as described in chapter 3; and (2) *deliberation* (slow consulting) vs. *delineation* (fast consulting)—as discussed in chapter 6. Both freedom and urgency are essential; intelligent organizations figure out the mix that works for them. Much of the challenge has to do with integrating autonomy and cooperation—as chapter 8 illustrates.

35. Ivar Ekeland, *Mathematics and the Unexpected* (Chicago: University of Chicago Press, 1988), 62–63.

36. Kevin Kelly, *Out of Control* (Reading, MA: Addison-Wesley, 1994), 401.

Chapter 8. A New Organizational Form

1. In fact, Thompson himself (*Organizations in Action*, New York: McGraw-Hill, 1967, 52) provided an early metaphor for autonomy/cooperation: the *synthetic organization*—an "*ad hoc* organization which usually emerges to overcome the effects of large-scale natural disasters in communities (at least in modern industrialized societies)." To put this hybrid in historical perspective, more than one-hundred years ago the English philosopher Herbert Spencer advanced similar ideas for society as a whole: "by the early 1880s . . . [his] social philosophy, and particularly his views on self-reliance and the minimal role of government in the life of the citizen, had become popular in the United States, where they were widely regarded as fitting the American democratic ideal of a nation of freely cooperating individuals unhindered by an interfering state" (Kevin Nute, *Frank Lloyd Wright and Japan* [New York: Van Nostrand Reinhold, 1993], 74).

2. John Van Maanen, "An Interview with John Van Maanen," Academy of Management *Organization and Management Theory Division Newsletter*, Winter 1994, 1.

3. James P. Womack and Daniel T. Jones, "From Lean Production to the Lean Enterprise," *Harvard Business Review*, March-April 1994, 103.

4. Lucien Rhodes, "The Un-Manager," *Inc.*, August 1982, 34.

5. Bill Gore, quoted by Rhodes, *op. cit.*, 36.

6. "Virtual" has also been applied to *tribes* (John Naisbitt, *Global Paradox* [New York: Morrow, 1994]); to the concept of *leadership* (John Huey, "The New Post-Heroic Leadership," *Fortune*, February 21, 1994, 42–44, 48, 50); and to *families, villages*, and *cities* (Charles Handy, *The Age of Paradox* [Boston: Harvard Business School Press, 1994]).

7. There are, to be sure, limits on locational freedom, as noted by an essay in *The Economist* ("Concentrating the Minds," May 21, 1994, 15): "Not everything can happen on line: Geography will have its due. A technological researcher cannot, unless he works entirely in virtual worlds, do his job just anywhere. The complex mixture of social, mental and physical skills that makes laboratory science work requires equipment and exper-

tise all in one place, however quaint that may come to seem to free-floaters in corporate finance. And the net cannot yet provide the fantastically flexible labour markets of true science cities. A researcher in Silicon Valley has hundreds of potential jobs within reach of his house; a researcher in Plains, Georgia, may not, however deeply he is plugged in."

8. Steve Jobs, quoted by George Gendron and Bo Burlingame (eds.) in "The Entrepreneur of the Decade," *Inc.*, April 1989, 116.

9. Jim Manzi, "Computer Keiretsu: Japanese Idea, U.S. Style," *The New York Times*, February 6, 1994, F15.

10. "The Bit Business," Television Survey, *The Economist*, February 12, 1994, 7.

11. Donald A. Norman, *Things that Make Us Smart* (Reading, MA: Addison-Wesley, 1993), 179.

12. *Ibid.*, 180. This state of affairs appears to be in flux. In spring 1994, Lotus Notes stood out as the autonomy/cooperation leader in groupware. According to Laurie Flynn in "How Lotus Is Raising the Level of Group Dynamics" (*The New York Times*, April 10, 1994, 16F): "Most software that calls itself groupware focuses on a single discrete task, like group scheduling or document editing. Notes, by contrast, is the Swiss Army Knife of groupware—a software package that allows corporate programmers to create applications to handle any of hundreds of workgroup tasks. . . . It lets customers take a rather free-form approach to creating network data bases. . . . It is a marked departure from traditional relational data bases, in which information is structured in a fixed format and relationships between various pieces of information are set and inflexible."

13. See, for example, the account of ADP's sales meetings, known internally as "roll call," in Donald K. Clifford, Jr. and Richard E. Cavanagh, *The Winning Performance* (New York: Bantam, 1985), 197.

14. David E. Sanger, "At Japan Inc., The Melody Changes, The Harmony Stays," *The New York Times*, May 6, 1990, E3.

15. David L. Bradford and Allan R. Cohen, "Post-Heroic Leadership," Letters to *Fortune, Fortune*, March 21, 1994, 29. Bradford and Cohen wrote *Managing for Excellence* (New York: Wiley, 1984).

16. Jonathan Hale, *The Old Way of Seeing* (Boston: Houghton Mifflin, 1994), 106. The matter is put more bluntly by Donald W. Hoppen in *The Seven Ages of Frank Lloyd Wright* (Santa Barbara: Capra Press, 1993), 171: "Arthur Drexler said, 'A skyscraper is a machine for making money.' Today . . . developers compress more and more boxes into high density structures. The box has become even more sterile, and man seems fated to spend his life living, working (and terminating) in a box. The horizontal ghetto is upended into the vertical tower. [Frank Lloyd] Wright called it, 'The sanitary slum.'"

17. Hoppen, *op. cit.*, 49.

18. Tom Peters, *Liberation Management* (New York: Knopf, 1992), 11.

19. Alan Deutschman, "How H-P Continues To Grow and Grow," *Fortune*, May 2, 1994, 90–92, 96, 98, 100.

20. Ronald Henkoff, "Getting Beyond Downsizing," *Fortune*, January 10, 1994, 58–60, 62, 64.

21. The following account draws substantially from David Kirkpatrick, "Could AT&T Rule the World?" *Fortune*, May 17, 1993, 55–57, 62–64, 66; and AT&T's *1993 Annual Report*.

22. Personal communication with Diana Thompson, Division Manager, Critical Issues, AT&T, April 8, 1994.

23. AT&T, *1993 Annual Report*, 9.

24. Personal communication with Burke Stinson, AT&T Corporate Media Relations Manager, January 21, 1994.

25. Kirkpatrick, *op. cit.*, 66.

26. Personal communication with Diana Thompson, Division Manager, Critical Issues, AT&T, April 8, 1994.

27. Douglas Merchant and Ruthann Prange, "Resource Link: A Vehicle for Providing Continuity at AT&T," in Peter M. Senge, Charlotte Roberts, Richard B. Ross, Bryan J. Smith, and Art Kleiner, *The Fifth Discipline Fieldbook* (New York: Doubleday Currency, 1994), 524.

28. Hesh Kestin, *21st Century Management* (New York: Atlantic Monthly Press, 1992), 131.

29. *Ibid.*, 166.

30. Rich Karlgaard, "ASAP Interview: Charles Wang," *Forbes ASAP*, April 11, 1994, 57–59.

31. Personal communication with Charles Wang, chairman, Computer Associates, April 22, 1994.

32. Computer Associates International, Inc., *1993 Annual Report*, 13.

33. Kestin, *op. cit.*, 119.

34. Francis Fukuyama, quoted by Jay Branegan in "Is Singapore a Model for the West?" *Time*, January 18, 1993, 36.

35. Charles Handy , *op. cit.,* 89, quotes Arthur Okun as follows: "the 'invisible hand' needs to be accompanied by an 'invisible handshake.'" Handy goes on to argue that "Unbalanced self-interest can only lead to an environment in which any victory will mean destroying those on whom our own survival will ultimately depend. That would be, literally, the paradox to end all paradoxes. The tragedy of the commons, it was labeled, when individual farmers maximized their own short-term use of the common land only to find that, when everyone did the same, the land deteriorated until all grazing failed."

36. Christopher Alexander, *A Foreshadowing of 21st Century Art* (New York: Oxford, 1993), 36.

37. Two useful overviews of complexity theory are M. Mitchell Waldrop, *Complexity: The Emerging Science at the Edge of Order and Chaos* (New York: Simon & Schuster, 1992); and Roger Lewin, *Complexity: Life at the Edge of Chaos* (New York: Macmillan, 1992). In a review of both books in *Science,* January 1993, 387–88, chemistry professor Lionel G. Harrison says, "I read Lewin's book second of the pair, and almost felt that I was watching the film of Waldrop's book."

38. Patricia Churchland, quoted by Lewin, *op. cit.,* 164.

39. John H. Holland, quoted by Waldrop, *op. cit.,* 145. Holland's observations find expression socially in present-day Japan, according to David Allen, a fellow at Harvard's Kennedy School of Government. In a letter to *The New York Times* ("Competition, the Japanese Way," September 13, 1992, F15), Allen writes that "Competition itself is defined in dramatically different ways. In the United States, wishing a business competitor ill is simply part of standard economic warfare. In Japan, commercial contention is, if anything, more intense. But getting ahead means doing the best possible work. The emphasis is productive, not destructive. And the welfare of all is integral to the formula. If a company gets into trouble, competitors may even help. Japan manages to have the advantages of both intense competition *and* ties among fellow voyagers on the economic boat."

40. Chris Langton, quoted by Lewin, *op. cit.,* 190.

41. Waldrop, *op. cit.,* 255.

42. Barbara Braun, *Pre-Columbian Art and the Post-Columbian World* (New York: Abrams, 1993). In the same vein, M.C. Escher resonated with the canons of J.S. Bach, who in Escher's opinion "played with repetition, superposition, inversion, mirroring, acceleration and slowing down of his themes in a way which is, in many regards comparable with my translation and glide-mirroring of my 'themes' of recognizable figures. And that's perhaps why I love his music particularly" (quoted by Doris Schattschneider in *Visions of Symmetry* [New York: W.H. Freeman, 1990], 254).

43. E.L. Trist, G.W. Higgin, H. Murray, and A.B. Pollock, *Organizational Choice: Capabilities of Groups at the Coal Face under Changing Technologies* (London: Tavistock, 1963). See also E.L. Trist and K.W. Bamforth, "Some Social and Psychological Consequences of the Longwall Method of Coal-Getting," *Human Relations, 4,* 1965, 3–38.

44. See, for example, "Precedents to Systems Theory," which includes essays by A. Angyal, and by J. Feibleman & J.W. Friend, in F.E. Emery (ed.), *Systems Thinking* (Harmondsworth, Middlesex, England: Penguin Books, 1969).

45. Ernest Fenollosa, quoted by Kevin Nute, in *Frank Lloyd Wright and Japan* (New York: Van Nostrand Reinhold, 1993), 76.

Appendix A. Notes on Design Methods

1. According to an Accountemps-sponsored survey of 200 senior-level corporate managers, the typical executive spends the equivalent of two months per year in unnecessary meetings (cited in *Boardroom Reports*, September 15, 1990, 15).

2. See, for example, Joseph McCann and Thomas N. Gilmore, "Diagnosing Organizational Decision Making through Responsibility Charting," *Sloan Management Review*, Winter 1983, 3–15; and Thomas N. Gilmore and Robert K. Kazanjian, "Clarifying Decision Making in High-Growth Ventures: The Use of Responsibility Charting," *Journal of Business Venturing, 4,* 1989, 69–83.

3. R.F. Vancil and C.H. Green, "How CEOs Use Top Management Committees," *Harvard Business Review*, January-February 1984, 65–73.

4. Noel M. Tichy and Stratford Sherman, *Control Your Destiny or Someone Else Will* (New York: Doubleday Currency, 1993), 27.

5. Tim Smart, "Wall Street's Bitter Lessons for GE," *Business Week*, August 22, 1994, 62.

INDEX

CPSIA information can be obtained
at www.ICGtesting.com
Printed in the USA
LVHW051241050619
620202LV00001B/223/P

9 781587 982590